Guided Research in Middle School
Mystery in the Media Center

LaDawna Harrington
Foreword by Dr. Carol C. Kuhlthau
Illustrated by Rachael Harrington

Linworth
Books

**Professional Development Resources for
K-12 Library Media and Technology Specialists**

Permissions

Thank you to Joyce Valenza for writing the script "Why Take Notes." I have adapted the script by permission of the American Library Association from the 1998 edition of *Power Tools*. Thank you Rachael Harrington for brilliANTly illustrating this book. Thank you Matthew Harrington for writing the *Case of the Salty Pickerel*, which I use to introduce students to ways to look for clues within a text.

Library of Congress Cataloging-in-Publication Data

Harrington, LaDawna.
  Guided research in middle school : mystery in the media center / LaDawna Harrington ; illustrated by Rachael Harrington.
      p. cm.
  Includes bibliographical references.
  ISBN 1-58683-221-2 (pbk.)
  1. Study skills--Handbooks, manuals, etc. 2. Report writing--Handbooks, manuals, etc. 3. Instructional materials centers--Research--Methodology.
I. Title.
  LB1601.H37 2007
  371.3'0281--dc22

                        2006021289

Cynthia Anderson: Acquisitions Editor
Carol Simpson: Editorial Director
Judi Repman: Consulting Editor

Published by Linworth Publishing, Inc.
480 East Wilson Bridge Road, Suite L
Worthington, Ohio 43085

ISBN: 1-58683-221-2

FSC
Mixed Sources
Product group from well-managed
forests and other controlled sources
Cert no. SW-COC-002283
www.fsc.org
© 1996 Forest Stewardship Council

5 4 3 2

Table of Contents

About the Author. v

Acknowledgements v

Foreword. vi

Introduction. viii
    Building the Anthill: The Guided Research Process x
    Curriculum Connections xi

Unit Summary and Basic Lessons Taught 1
    Guided Research. 1
    Research Model 1
    Unit Organization Example 4
    Unit Organization Template 5

Lesson 1:   Keywords in Action 6
    Handout: Pretest/Posttest 8

Lesson 2:   Just the Facts Ma'am 10
    Note Taking Skit. 13
    Handout: The Case of the Salty Pickerel 15

Lesson 3:   Becoming a Good Detective. 16
    PowerPoint 18

Lesson 4:   What Is the Concept? 24
    Transparency: Mystery Concept Map 26
    Mystery Topic List 27

Lesson 5:   It Is No Beef, Just Boolean. 29
    Nothing Is Something. 31
    Transparency: Topic Concept Map. 32
    Transparency: Building the Pyramid 33
    Transparency: Boolean Logic Map 33

Lesson 6:   Making Your Statement 34

Lesson 7:   Amazing Tools 37
    Reference/Nonfiction Assessment 39
    Electronic Sources Assessment 40
    Print Media Assessment 41

Lesson 8:   Direction By Reflection 42

Lesson 9:   Giving Credit Where Credit Is Due 44
    Theories Web 46

Lesson 10: Untangling the Web 47

Lesson 11: Linking It All Together 49

Lesson 12: And Now Presenting 51
    Outline Example 54
    Sample Note Card. 55
    Oral Speaking Rubric 56

Table of Contents continued

Handout: Speaker's Rubric 57

Evaluating the Casebook Rubric 58

Unit Evaluation Rubric 59

Mini-Lesson Worksheets (Research Planning Worksheet/Being

ObservANT) 61

Handout: Preparing Your Oral Presentation 63

Promotion Certificate 66

Detective's Casebook 67

Recommended Reading 99

Table of Figures

Figure 1:   Anthill Table 67, 98

Figure 2:   Unit Organization Example 4

Figure 3:   Unit Organization Template 5

Figure 4:   Pretest Area of the Library 9

PowerPoint Slides (12 slides word doc) 18

Figure 5:   Mystery Concept Map 26

Figure 6:   Pyramid Example 30

Figure 7:   Topic Concept Map 32, 74

Figure 8:   Pyramid 33, 75

Figure 9:   Boolean Logic 33

Figure 10: Ref Non Fic Assessment 39

Figure 11: Electronic Sources Assessment 40

Figure 12: Print Media Assessment 41

Figure 13: Theories Web 46

Figure 14: Outline Example 54

Figure 15: Sample Note Card 55

Figure 16: Oral Speaking Rubric 56

Figure 17: Speaker Rubric 57

Figure 18: Evaluating the Casebook Rubric 58

Figure 19: Unit Evaluation Rubric 59

Figure 20: Research Planning Worksheet 61

Figure 21: Being ObservANT 62

Figure 22: Promotion Certificate 66

Figure 23: Nothing Is Something 69

Figure 24: Tools of the Trade 70

Figure 25: Area of the Library 70

Figure 26: Hunt for Answers Checklist 77

Figure 27: Reference Citation Table 78

Figure 28: Nonfiction Citation Table 81

Figure 29: Making Your Statement 85

Figure 30: Database Citation Table 86

Figure 31: Internet Citation Table 89

Figure 32: Web Evaluation 92

Figure 33: Periodical Citation Table 93

Illustrations

Illustration 1: Detective Ant . . . . .Front Cover, viii, xii, 9, 10, 18, 23, 39, 40, 41, 62, 66, 67, 68

Illustration 2: Brainiac Ant 20, 34, 85

Illustration 3: Nervous Ant 52

Illustration 4: Carpenter Ant 1

Illustration 5: Spy Ant 4, 5, 16, 18, 22, 61, 70

Illustration 6: Key 6

Illustration 7: Anthill 6, 10, 16, 22, 29, 34, 37, 42, 44, 47, 49, 51

Illustration 8: Footprints 13, 15, 18, 23, 28, 92

Illustration 9: Graphic Organizer Ant 24

Illustration 10: Matador Ant 29

Illustration 11: Ant Maze 37, 69

Illustration 12: Zero Ant 42

Illustration 13: Apple Ant 44

Illustration 14: Knotted Up Ant 47

Illustration 15: Teacher Ant 51

Illustration 16: Public Speaking Ant 64, 65

Illustration 17: Question Ant 19, 21, 27, 69, 96, 97

Illustration 18: Direction by Reflection 96

Illustration 19: Ant Carrying Key 97

About the Author

LaDawna Harrington received a B.A. in Speech Communications and Dramatic Arts from the University of Northern Colorado and a Master's of Library Science from Rutgers, The State University of New Jersey. She has been active in the New Jersey Association of School Librarians serving as President, and in 2004 received the New Jersey Library Media Specialist of the Year Award. Her school was one of 10 schools chosen in New Jersey to participate in a pilot study done by the Center for International Scholarship in School Libraries to track the impact of a good school library program on student learning.

Acknowledgments

The inquiry process found in this book was developed because Ann Boyle, my creative and flexible colleague, let me create and recreate this process with her students over several years. My gratitude goes to Dr. Carol C. Kuhlthau who taught me the power of collaboration and to use inquiry to guide students into research. Thanks to Pam Chesky, my supervisor, who encouraged me to try new ways of teaching. I also want to thank the supportive people at Linworth, especially Marlene Woo-Lun, Cynthia Anderson, Donna King, and Sherry York, who have patiently helped this first time author through the process.

Most of all I want to thank my family. Matt, who knew I needed to be a teacher and gave me wings to become one. Taylor and Rachael, who practically went to grad school with me so that I could become a librarian. Thanks Rachael for doing the artwork that fills the pages of this book. Love to Mom and Dad for their way of guiding me to think and be creative. You guys are my real inspiration.

Foreword

Over the years that I have been teaching in the Masters in Library and Information Science Degree Program at Rutgers University, I have noticed that people drawn to working with middle school students have some things in common. They have a delightful sense of humor, thoroughly enjoy being with students, and take a creative approach to their work. LaDawna Harrington is among the most gifted of my former students and exemplifies the best of middle school librarianship. Her background in business, theater, and education brings an unusual richness to her work in the middle school library. When she first became a middle school librarian, nearly 10 years ago, she immediately set out to collaborate with teachers in her school to create her innovative inquiry approach to research. It was a resounding success with students, teachers, and her principal.

Recently, LaDawna's school was selected as one of the sites in the Rutgers University Center for International Scholarship in School Libraries (CISSL) study of the Impact of School Libraries on Student Learning, funded by the Institute for Museum and Library Studies (IMLS). Student learning in that middle school library media center was among the highest in the study. Many of the inquiry strategies employed in that study are incorporated in this book.

One of LaDawna Harrington's most successful collaborations is the mystery unit to guide students through research that she presents in this book. She has continued to test, adapt, and change this unit responding to students' needs and the latest advances in information technology. She has regularly shared her expertise with the students in my Masters courses, and I have urged her to publish her ideas to share with other school librarians as well. This book clearly describes the steps of motivating and guiding middle school students in inquiry learning through the school library for you to use and adapt for your students.

LaDawna Harrington has based this book on several important premises:

- First, although middle school students need constant guiding through the research process, what she calls a research apprenticeship, middle school students are also at an age when they want to separate and be independent. LaDawna is sensitive to these seemingly conflicting needs and provides continual guidance that leads to confidence and independence, without being overly intrusive.

- Second, imagination is a powerful motivator for middle school students. LaDawna develops information literacy and problem solving skills through creative fun and imaginative role-playing.

- Third, middle school students are at an ideal age to develop expertise in searching. Search skills and strategies are introduced and developed throughout the research process in this inquiry unit. For example, identifying new keywords as the research progresses facilitates subject access.

- Fourth, middle school students learn by thinking deeply about their work. LaDawna provides opportunities for reflection that are integrated into the research process.

- Fifth, assessment is an essential element in any learning process. Pretests and posttests are provided to document learning with a recommendation that the posttest be given after some time has passed to determine what students retain.

In *Guided Research in Middle School: Mystery in the Media Center*, LaDawna combines her expertise for practical application of theory with her exceptional understanding of this grade level. It is a challenging way for middle school students to develop information literacy and have fun solving problems through inquiry in the school library.

Carol Collier Kuhlthau, Professor II Emerita
Library and Information Science, Rutgers,
The State University of New Jersey
Director, Center for International Scholarship
in School Libraries (CISSL)

Introduction

We are all looking for the "hook" that will engage our students and make them want to learn. A little imagination, a little drama, a little mystery and the students are hooked. This book uses role-playing and mystery to snag students into a problem-solving, inquiry-based process that culminates with students being able to form opinions and make sense of their own ways of thinking. Students are equipped with strategies to structure their own search process.

I teach students ages 10-14, a crucial time in the development of problem-solving, critical-thinking, and organizational abilities. At this age, children are highly impressionable, acquiring much of their learning through imitation. They have an extraordinary need to explore and do things for themselves. They are living in a paradox, struggling to find their place in the world while at the same time trying to disconnect from those who can help them find that place. Understanding this stage of development should have a profound impact on how we teach in the middle school classroom. Teachers can be invaluable in helping students gain understanding about their own thinking, or ways of thinking.

I needed to develop an inquiry process that would guide my students to make inferences and to explore ideas. I wanted to help my students discover by questioning. I wanted to provide tools that would enable them to make sense of their evolving organizational abilities and their beginning efforts to think critically to solve problems. My students want to be empowered with things that I can teach them, but they also have an overwhelming desire to think for themselves. Understanding my students' struggles has helped in the development of this inquiry process. This process can be described as a research apprenticeship. An apprentice is someone who learns from a mentor who walks beside them, encouraging them to question. Questions, are not usually answered by the mentor, but instead are responded to with guidance to help the apprentice gain knowledge, make judgments, and come to conclusions.

This book is broken into two sections. The first section describes lessons, strategies, information standards, and materials you will need to teach the lessons. The second portion of the book is a student casebook. The casebook is designed to guide the students to ask themselves questions, and to find solutions as they gather information from the many resources of the library media center. All pages from this portion of the book are reproducible and can be copied as needed.

As a student in Dr. Carol C. Kuhlthau's classes at Rutgers University, I was introduced to her Information Search Process model on the affective aspect of research. This way of thinking about how kids approach research touched a chord with me as I began to explore the idea of creative thinking and role-playing. I felt that creativity in children could be an approach to connecting them to critical thinking skills that would help them overcome the anxious feelings they may have through the research process. This casebook has been developed and adapted over time as I have gained experience working with middle school students and wonderful colleagues like Ann Boyle and Jessica Plesniak.

In order to ignite imagination and creativity the students become detectives researching their own mystery topic, teachers become captains, and the library media center becomes information headquarters. Students use the casebook to record important clues about assigned mysteries. This role-playing strategy is a motivating tool because the imagination is turned on as students take ownership. They engage in something in which they feel they are an active part.

Today's students are already used to role-playing in digital environments. The gaming industry is booming because these games require engagement and play that allows for construction and reconstruction of solutions to problems. Role-playing is the kind of engagement that has been used to connect for centuries. The digital environment is just a different format. What students really want is to be a part of what is going on. Through purposeful play, creative thinking and problem-solving skills develop.

During this project the teacher and library media specialist will guide the students through their casebooks by using the teacher's section. There are 12 lessons that can be done using a flexible library schedule over an entire marking period, or condensed into blocks of time, depending on local curriculum or time structures. When the investigative process comes to a close, the "detectives" draw conclusions about their mystery, give an oral presentation, and are promoted to "lieutenant" in a ceremony in which they receive a certificate.

This role-playing experience will have provided a step-by-step inquiry process by which students are engaged to think, rethink, organize, and develop problem-solving skills that will prepare them for the complex, information rich society in which we live. I call this process the Anthill because I want my students to learn to be observANT.

The **ANTHILL** process can easily be adapted for a variety of themes and research projects, because it is about role-playing, imagination, and process. An example might be researching ancient civilizations where all recorded history has been destroyed and having the students be time travelers who must go back in time to recreate the civilization as it was, recording what they discover about daily life so that future generations can know what life was once like. Or how about research on ocean life or a coral "reef" search where students become marine biologists as the hook for a science project.

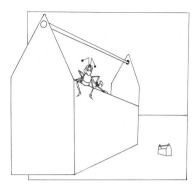

Building the Anthill: The Guided Research Process

What is the research process? How can we create an environment where students get excited about discovery?

Libraries today are active, vibrant places filled with many different source materials available in a wide variety of formats. There are so many information choices that the research process can be complicated and overwhelming. Students have so many choices and decisions to make. Middle school students want independence; however, they still need someone or something to provide them with strategies to sort through the vast amounts of materials they have access to.

Analyze. Students need to examine their mystery topic to gather ideas so that they can think about where to begin to look for answers. The students are taught to look at keywords and sentence structure. They start with what they know (SIK or "Stuff I Know") and then develop strategies to ask themselves what they need to know (SINK or "Stuff I Need to Know"). They need to ask themselves questions that will lead to discovery.

Nothing is something. Answers are not always obvious. Students can be guided to think of other ways to approach their topic. They need to learn to use synonyms or other words or phrases that might help them find answers. This provides opportunity to introduce broad and narrow categories.

Think of all your possibilities. The students are asked to develop "I wonder" statements to explore everything they want to find out about their topic before they set out to hunt for answers.

Hunt for answers. With casebook in hand the detectives begin gathering information. They are guided how to use indexes, the OPAC, and how to formulate good search statements to use when accessing electronic databases and the Internet. They are asked to record what works and does not work as they use keywords or phrases.

Isolate/Interpret. Students are instructed to stop and ask themselves, "Does the information I have gathered from this specific source answer my 'I wonder' statements and how will this help me form opinions?" They are asked to do this procedure for all the sources from which they access information.

Learn direction by reflection. About mid-way through the project the students are asked to pause and reflect on how their project is progressing. This pause gives both the students and the teachers an opportunity to make sure the process is working and that knowledge construction is taking place. It is an opportunity to learn from mistakes. Sometimes the mistakes are just what are needed to bring the project back into focus or to head in a different direction. Students need to take this time to think about their thinking—what worked, what did not work. This procedure will be done again on a larger scale at the end of the project.

Link it all together. It is time for students to take the information they have gathered and make sense out of it. They will be asked to form opinions and communicate what they have discovered about their topic.

Curriculum Connections

This guided research process can be implemented across the curriculum, but the topics need to be selected and the questions designed based on your library collection.

It is important to help students develop thinking skills and essential questions as they attack the research process. Essential questions require students to make decisions or plan a course of action. Most middle school students have not learned the strategies to develop essential questions and usually need help when they are first learning this skill. Writing essential questions takes patience and practice. Using unsolved mysteries guides the students to investigate a variety of theories and draw conclusions. The project in this book was designed for a language arts class but the mystery concept can be used in science, history, math, or any other curricular area. Really, mystery is a great hook for developing essential questions in any subject area, because it sets the stage for constructing questions that require forming opinions or a plan for finding a solution.

Students use brainstorming and concept mapping to develop ideas that they must write about. They read and interpret main ideas and author points of view and then compare information from various source materials while learning to take good concise notes. Synthesizing this information requires strategies that enable the students to write in varying forms for different audiences, contexts, and purposes. Communication and listening skills can be employed at the conclusion of the project using oral presentations, even videotaping the presentation to give to your local television network. This unit not only provides the mystery hook for implementing the inquiry process but also ignites enthusiasm for students to select a mystery novel of choice to read for enjoyment.

To start a cross-curricular project you will need to collaborate with the classroom teacher about what outcomes the teacher is seeking. Present the Anthill Research Model to the classroom teacher as a way of guiding students through their project. You will want to develop topic questions or a research scenario that will connect with the resources you have available. For instance, if you want to collaborate with a math teacher whose class is researching ancient mathematicians, you could have the students role-play being investigative reporters with the outcome a class newspaper. The newspaper would include classified ads, headline news, a food section, entertainment and the like, including a feature interview with the mathematician. As the students gather their information from the different areas of the library, you would follow the casebook by having them record their citations in the appropriate pages in the casebook and reflect by journaling about what information they have gathered from each of the sources. Oral presentation could be presented as the evening news based on the newspaper the class produces.

The research process presented in this book is just that, a process. It is a process by which you, as the teacher, can guide the students to ask questions, to be observant, and to be actively involved, while at the same time, a process that provides opportunity for modeling and intervention. School climates today are increasingly diverse in culture and language; mix with that the special needs child and children with differing ability levels and we have classrooms that must be flexible and lessons that can be easily developed or modified for multiple pathways to learning. We must be able to help young people make meaningful connections as they explore and make mistakes while building problem-solving skills to find solutions. This guided research unit allows for modification of lessons for a variety of topics and for differentiated instruction. You will find several examples in the teaching section of ways to modify the lessons for differing abilities. When teaching students from mixed ability classrooms, you need to build lessons for the highest level while providing individual support that may be needed by other students. My basic philosophy when developing this research unit was to walk beside students as their mentor. The very nature of this concept leads to flexibility for modification and individualized instruction. The design of this process is also very structured, and for children that are struggling, structure can help keep them on track and focused. This research process has been successfully implemented in collaboration with my colleague, Linda Malayter, a special education teacher. With Linda's insight into this special student population I have included several examples of how many of these lessons can be modified and adapted to meet the capabilities of individual students.

Working closely with the classroom teacher some lessons can be pre-taught. For instance, when the students are ready to hunt for answers, gather their information, and record their citations, a pre-lesson can be taught on how to find citation information in the book, database, or Web site. When teaching about keywords, broader and narrower topics, and "nothing is something," the classroom teacher could give lessons on synonyms and describing words. Another strategy for modification would be to teach several mini units that require one source at a time.

Unit Summary and Basic Lessons Taught

Guided Research

The keys to understanding (Lessons 1-3):
- Pretest: gain understanding of students' previous knowledge
- Note-taking skills: model through drama and a minute mystery story
- Highlighting strategies: copy, highlight, circle, and code
- PowerPoint: explain what it takes to be a good detective

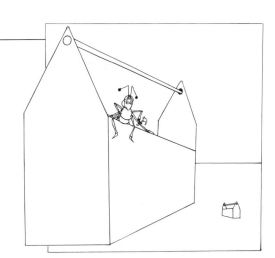

Research Model

- **A-Analyze**. Lessons 1-4. Lessons 1-3 are preparation for research. Establishing pre-knowledge, applying pre-knowledge, building strategies for attacking a problem.
- **N-Nothing is something**. Lesson 5. Understanding keywords and synonyms, and broad and narrow topics. When research seems to come to a dead end how can I help myself to find a solution?
- **T-Think of all your possibilities**. Lesson 6. Building "I Wonder" statements. Questions to ask that will lead to a solution or an action plan.

- **H-Hunt for answers**. Lesson 7. Locating and accessing information.
- **I-Isolate/Interpret**. Lesson 7. Interpreting information collected and tying to "I Wonder" statements.
- **L-Learn direction by reflection**. Lesson 8. Lessons learned, new strategies to take.
- **L-Linking it together**. Lessons 9-11. Citing work, plagiarism, outlining, cue cards, and presentation of final projects. Posttest (to evaluate knowledge gained).

Lesson 1: Keywords in Action

Time Frame: 1 class period

Administer the pretest. Take time to review and discuss the test. Explain the skills necessary for research, including the importance of keywords. As you go over the test you will discuss the importance of knowing that everything you do is research. Give an overview of the process and what will be expected for the final project. Explain that information will be gathered from four areas of the library, with citations from each. A three-minute oral presentation will be required with cue cards made from an outline of the research. A complete overview can be found in the student casebook on pages 67-98. Strategies for teaching on pages.

Lesson 2: Just the Facts Ma'am

Time Frame: 1-2 class periods

Note-taking skills will be modeled through drama and a story distributed to the students. Importance of keywords should be discussed and strategies for note taking stressing highlighting techniques.

Lesson 3: Becoming a Good Detective

Time Frame: 1 class period

Present the PowerPoint lesson. If you don't have the means to make your own slides using the slides included in this book on pages 18-23, you may make transparencies of the pages for an overhead projector. This lesson will reinforce keyword strategies and demonstrate mapping techniques that the students will use with their own topics.

Lesson 4: What Is the Concept?

Time Frame: 1 class period

Model concept mapping. Students will be given their individual topics during this lesson and they will map their topics. They will ask themselves questions about what they might already know about their topic. They will look for clues in their topic statement that might lead them to some understanding. They will also be encouraged to use encyclopedias and dictionaries to help them gain an overview of their topic.

Lesson 5: It Is No Beef, Just Boolean

Time Frame: 1 class period

Model stringing keywords into search strategies that make sense. Demonstrate using phrase searching, Boolean logic, and other searching techniques on the Internet, in databases, and in periodical indexes. Use the pyramid concept for organizing a topic in subject categories.

Lesson 6: Making Your Statement

Time Frame: 1 class period

Students will be guided to ask themselves pertinent questions about their research topic. The teacher will guide students to form essential questions to develop "I Wonder" statements about their topic.

Lesson 7: Amazing Tools

Time Frame: 5 class periods

The hunt begins. Students will now use the strategies they have learned to begin to gather their information from the various places in the library. As they gather information they will be implementing note-taking skills, making copies or printouts of their information, highlighting keywords, circling larger portions of text, coding significant clues, and writing in their casebooks about the information they are gathering.

Lesson 8: Direction By Reflection

Time Frame: 1 class period

Students are guided to reflect on what they have learned so far. What has worked and what has not. They are asked to stop, think, and write about their progress to this point. They may discover that they need to take a different direction or that they have new questions they need solved.

Lesson 9: Giving Credit Where Credit Is Due

Time Frame: 1 class period

Present a discussion of plagiarism and model how to build a bibliography from their citation worksheets.

Lesson 10: Untangling the Web

Time Frame: 1 class period

Model construction of a Web site, stressing the importance of evaluating the site in order to know that the information gathered is good.

Lesson 11: Linking It All Together

Time Frame: 1 class period

Using their casebooks, students will reflect on what they have learned.

Lesson 12: And Now Presenting

Time Frame: class periods will vary based on class size and how elaborate you get with your presentations and if you decide to film.

Students will make an outline of the information they have gathered, highlighted, and recorded. From the outline they will generate cue cards for the oral presentation they will give of their research topic. You may want to film their presentations and give them to the local television station.

Figure 2: Unit Organization Example

Organizing a Collaborative Unit

Unit: __Mystery in the Media Center__   Subject Area: __L.A.__   Grade: __6__   Classroom Teacher: ___

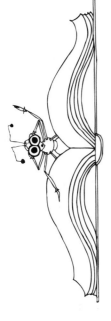

Lesson Objective	Time Frame	Location of Lesson	Materials	Core Curriculum Standards	Information Literacy Standards
LESSON 1 ▪ Discover previous knowledge ▪ Introduce unit	1 class period	Media Center	▪ Pretest ▪ Overhead projector/LCD	State Standards	1.1 1.2 1.5
LESSON 2 ▪ Identify important facts in a body of work ▪ Notetaking	1 class period	Media Center	▪ Script ▪ Transparency/white board ▪ Markers		1.1, 1.2, 1.3, 1.5 3.1, 3.2 6.2
LESSON 3 ▪ "Stuff I Know" ▪ PowerPoint ▪ Discovering strategies for beginning research	1 class period	Media Center	▪ Computer ▪ LCD projector ▪ PowerPoint ▪ Casebooks		1.1, 1.2, 1.3, 1.5 3.1, 3.2 6.2
LESSON 4 ▪ Task definition ▪ Concept Mapping ▪ Keywords, broad and narrow topics	1 class period	Media Center	▪ Transparencies/White board ▪ Overhead Projector ▪ Individual Topics ▪ Casebooks		1.1, 1.2, 1.3, 1.5 3.1, 3.2

Figure 3: Unit Organization Template

Organizing a Collaborative Unit

Subject Area: _____ Grade: _____ Classroom Teacher: _____

Unit: _____

Lesson Objective	Time Frame	Location of Lesson	Materials	Core Curriculum Standards	Information Literacy Standards

Lesson 1: Keywords in Action

Overview

Life is about problem solving. Students must come to understand that they do research in their everyday lives, from finding the phone number to order pizza, to deciding what movie they will see with their friends on Friday night. These are problem-solving skills, the springboard of research. Students need to learn how to place their specific ideas and needs into larger categories, subjects, and families. Example: to find information about the telephone they need to think about what family, or subject category, the telephone belongs to (communications), and then about communications— not public speaking or advertising—but electronic communications. This is extremely complex thinking. The teacher needs to model these skills by thinking out loud and in turn helping the students to think out loud.

Information Literacy Standards:

Standard 1: Indicators 1, 2, 5

★ Objectives:

Students will be able to:

Understand skills necessary for research, including the importance of keywords for knowing where and how to begin doing research.

Materials:

- Pretest
- Overhead projector
- Transparency (Pretest)
- Transparency markers

Strategies:

Give pretest found on pages 8-9

Before students begin investigating their individual mystery topics they are given a pretest to assess problem-solving capabilities. The pretest is the same for every student. They are asked to do the best that they can, with the understanding that this test will not be graded. Most of the students will know nothing about the mystery topic that is given in the pretest. That is okay. What is being looked at is whether the students can use sentence clues and keywords to construct meaning. The test topic is: What happened to cause the crew to mysteriously disappear from the Mary Celeste? The students are asked to write three facts in complete sentences about what they know about the topic just from the question. Some of the answers are: "Mary Celeste is not a person." "The Mary Celeste might be a boat or plane." "A crew has disappeared." Discussion about how we know these things ensues. As the test is reviewed, use of reference materials, like encyclopedias and biographical dictionaries, are demonstrated. When using an encyclopedia it is stressed that the index is the place to begin or the searcher might give up before getting started. Ask the students what keyword you should look under in the index. Some students will say Celeste, Mary. Some will say Mary; some will say ship. Show the students that if you go right to the C volume you will find nothing; if you go to the M volume you will find lots of Mary's, but not the Mary you are looking for. If you go to the S volume there are so many entries for "ship" that it makes finding the Mary Celeste difficult. Demonstrate that if you go to the index and look under Mary, you will be directed to the S volume under Ships, Famous and further narrowing under Mystery Ships. By demonstrating this process students begin to understand the thinking process you are using. This will help them as they begin implementing strategies for launching their own investigations. The important factor to stress is the gathering of clues by looking at keywords and sentence structure. This process will be reinforced in lesson three using the PowerPoint slides available.

Go over pretest found on pages 8-9 (make a transparency). Discuss the importance of knowing that everything you do is research and by knowing this you can begin to break down your topic to get at a starting point.

Introduce mystery unit. Give an overview of what the students will be doing during this research process and what is expected of them for a final project. A quick overview can be found in the student casebook on pages 67-71.

Build enthusiasm by introducing yourself as captain, referring to the students as detectives, and the library media center as information headquarters.

✔ Evaluation:

- Pretest results
- Observe students' understanding of research through in-class discussion as you go over the pretest

Name: _____ Class: _____

Describe how you would look for information in an encyclopedia about the mysterious disappearance of the crew on the Mary Celeste.

_____

_____

Describe how you would look for information using a search engine on the Internet or an online magazine database about the mysterious disappearance of the crew on the Mary Celeste.

_____

_____

Look at the question below and circle the keywords.

What happened to cause the crew to mysteriously disappear from the Mary Celeste?
Make a list of your keywords:

_____

_____

Research requires you to be observ**ANT.**
Analyze, ask yourself questions. What do you know about your topic already?
(SIK= "Stuff I Know")
Write three complete sentences of things you already know about the topic above.

_____

_____

_____

Circle the keywords in the above sentences.

Make a list of your keywords from the sentences above.

_____

_____

Look at the keywords you have listed. Use them in a search statement for searching on the Internet.

_____

_____

_____

_____

_____

Remember, in order to be a good detective you must be observ.ANT.

Analyze, ask yourself questions (SIK="Stuff I Know").
Nothing is something.

Look at the keywords you have circled above and think about those words. What would happen if you searched using those words and nothing worked out for you? Think of other words you could use instead of those words that would help you get information on this topic. List the new words you thought of below.

T=think of all your possibilities (SINK="Stuff I Need to Know").
What do I want to find out? Where will I look?
Fill in the chart below.

Figure 2: Pretest Area of the Library

Area of the Library Media Center (LMC)	Tools to Use in Each Area

Lesson 2: Just the Facts Ma'am

Overview

Inside the mystery scene there are important decisions to make. There are clues all around that may be easy for a detective to miss unless he knows what he is looking for. At times there will be too much information, while at other times it will seem that clues for solving the case are elusive. Decisions may not be easy to make. A good detective must be observANT. Getting a focus is the most difficult aspect of research, because research is not a linear process. It is a gathering process. It is a thinking process that requires analysis, nothing is something, thinking of possibilities, hunting for answers, having a feeling of "I can succeed" by isolating facts and interpreting those facts to make new knowledge, learning from mistakes by reflection to give new direction, and finally linking everything together.

Information Literacy Standards:

Standard 1: Indicators 1, 2, 3, 5
Standard 3: Indicators 1, 2
Standard 6: Indicator 2

★ Objectives:

Students will be able to:

- Identify important facts in a body of work
- Highlight, circle, and code important facts in a body of work in order to record their research

Copy

Make a working copy of information in order to highlight, circle, and code important information. A copy might be photocopied material from a book or a printout of information gathered from the Internet or a database. Copying the material allows for resource sharing and detours plagiarism because the copy will be reviewed by the teacher to look for highlighting strategies, making sure students understand how to look for keywords and concepts.

   (This method to teach note taking has been in my repertoire for more than 10 years and was learned from a student research guideline manual prepared by my school district some years ago. The earlier version was replaced in 1997. This new version does not include these same strategies for teaching note taking, nor is it available any longer. However, I still use this method because the connection between keywords on print and transferring that thinking process to the electronic environment has proven to be very successful.)

Highlight

Students should be taught the importance of highlighting keywords *only* in their body of information.

Circle

When an entire paragraph is important, the student should circle that paragraph instead of highlighting the paragraph because, again, we are trying to teach keywords and their significance. Within the circled paragraph there may be keywords that should be highlighted.

Code

A star, a checkmark, an asterisk, or some other code of choice can be used for information such as dates, names, etc. that will be included in the final presentation. Each of the source materials will be turned in with the bibliography.

Materials:

- Mystery role-playing script (adapted from *Power Tools* by Joyce Valenza by permission of the American Library Association)
- Costumes and props as desired
- Blank transparencies for note taking
- Transparency markers
- Overhead projector
- Smart board or white board (if you have these they are the technology of choice)
- *Case of the Salty Pickerel* (minute mystery: copy one for each student and make a transparency that you will use on the projector to demonstrate the strategy of highlighting, circling, and coding)

Strategies:

The inquiry process is kicked off with a skit presented by the media specialist and the classroom teacher. The skit, found on pages 13-14, demonstrates understanding how to take notes, identifying keywords in a text, and recording concise facts. As the skit is performed, the students will see that it is impossible for the Inspector to write down everything that Ms. Holcomb is trying to report. They will learn that not everything that is being said is necessary to record. The students learn that by recording just the facts the entire scenario can be reconstructed using only brief notes and keywords. The skit is followed up by having the students read through a minute mystery to identify keywords.

Introduce note-taking skills by having students highlight, circle, and code important facts from their copy of the *Case of the Salty Pickerel* (minute mystery handout) to crack the case. An overhead transparency and a walk-through-the-minute mystery will demonstrate what is important and what is ancillary. By using the tools of the trade (like all good detectives), the students are taught that when they have a question, something they cannot define, they must find solutions to solve their problem. Let them know that it is important to clarify anything in the story they do not understand. Allow students time to work on their own as they try to solve the mystery. Dictionaries should be placed on the tables for students' use as they read through the minute mystery. Use a transparency of the story to demonstrate how to highlight, circle, and code as you go over the story with the students. If you have a white board or smart board you will have a copy posted, and then demonstrate highlighting keywords and circling longer passages that are important. By discussing the fact that they cannot crack the case unless they identify unknown words and terms, you are guiding them to find solutions around obstacles that might block them from completing their task. By looking up the word pickerel (which most of the students will not know) they discover that a pickerel is a fresh water fish. They are learning to be observANT. They are learning to look for clues while using tools to solve problems. They have cracked their first case and are on their way to active, engaged involvement.

✔ Evaluation:

Observe students' reactions to telephone conversation from role-playing. Have students reconstruct the entire scene from the second note-taking scenario when the inspector is recording just the facts. The notes on the transparency or smart board should be few and brief, showing the students that they can retell the scene just from the key points, something they will need to do for their final project when they present a three-minute oral presentation.

Review students' use of note-taking procedures on their minute mysteries. After you have allowed time for the students to highlight, use dictionaries, code, and write down their solution to the case, discuss several conclusions. Allow students time to respond. If no one has figured out what a pickerel is, then lead them to the fact that they must use dictionaries when they don't understand terms. Collect the minute mysteries and review for highlighting, circling, and coding skills. Solving the case is less important than getting the concept of highlighting just the important information.

▶▶ Extensions:

- Use newspapers to reinforce searching for keywords and taking notes. The classroom teacher should be constantly reinforcing keywords in passages and highlighting only those keywords (not complete text).
- Identify keywords in paragraphs from literature texts. Short story handouts may be distributed and then students may highlight only keywords in the text. Ask students to find main ideas and supporting details.

Note Taking Skit

(Adapted by permission of the American Library Association from the 1998 edition of *Power Tools* by Joyce Valenza.)

Objective: To learn the importance of taking brief, significant notes. The lesson requires a cooperating teacher who will role-play with you. Tell the students that you are making a phone call to report a missing person to the chief inspector's headquarters. As the scene ensues the inspector will use transparency markers to record the conversation on a transparency that will be used to project for the students to see. The inspector should try and write down everything. Because it will be impossible for the inspector to write as fast as Ms. Holcomb speaks, the inspector will have to interrupt the conversation several times asking Ms. Holcomb to please repeat what she just said.

Characters:

Chief Inspector Watts
Ms. Marlena Holcomb

Setting the Scene:

The teacher stands at one end of the room and the LMS at the other. The LMS, using an imaginary phone, keys in a phone number. The phone rings and the "inspector" picks up.

WATTS: Watts here.

MARLENA: Yes, is this Chief Inspector Watts?

WATTS: That's right, may I help you?

MARLENA: Oh, Inspector Watts, this is Marlena Holcomb. Inspector, I need to report a missing person.

WATTS: A missing person? Yes, well go on. (The inspector begins to take notes on the transparency trying to write down everything as Marlena begins to unfold her story.)

MARLENA: Inspector you must investigate this missing person. I have reason to believe she is not only missing but may in fact be dead.

WATTS: Dead you say? Go on Ms. Uh??? Ms. Uh??

MARLENA: Marlena Holcomb.

WATTS: Yes. Ms. Holcomb, please continue.

MARLENA: Yes, I'd like to report that Mrs. Jean Neimann was last seen on February 11th. Inspector I am a professional actor and I belong to the Actor's Equity. I work with Mrs. Neimann who is also a member. Or maybe I should say that I worked with Mrs. Neimann. You see I haven't seen Jean since February 11. Mrs. Neimann performs under the names of Lora Fay and Victoria Taylor. The nature of her disappearance has led me to make some of my own investigations.

WATTS: Go on. (Watts continues interrupting to take notes.)

MARLENA: Yes well...Let's see, Yes...um...it seems that Mr. And Mrs. Robert Wayne were guests of the Neimann's on the night of January 31. According to the Waynes, Mr. and Mrs. Neimann had a brief quarrel that evening and on February 19 the Actor's Association received a letter from Mrs. Neimann saying she had to leave immediately to attend to sick relatives in Colorado.

WATTS: Not too out of the ordinary do you think Ms. Holcomb?

MARLENA: But Inspector, I looked at the letter. It was not written in Jean's handwriting and the other day, I saw Dr. Neimann in public with Miss Rachael Davis, his secretary. I also found out that Miss Davis has taken moved into Dr. Neimann's home. That was on March 12.

WATTS: Yes, seems a little fishy. Well Ms. Holcomb I will check into this case. Please call me if you think of anything else.

MARLENA: Yes, Inspector. Thank you, I will. (Marlena hangs up the phone and immediately realizes that she has forgotten to tell the Inspector something else and dials the phone again.)

WATTS: Inspector Watts here.

MARLENA: Oh yes Inspector, one other thing.

WATTS: Yes, is this Ms. Holcomb?

MARLENA: Oh yes Inspector, sorry.

WATTS: Yes, well, Ms. Holcomb maybe you should start from the very beginning as I think I will be bringing this report under full investigation.

MARLENA: Yes, OK, but Inspector, one more thing, about 12 days after Miss Davis moved in with Dr. Neimann, I received a black-bordered announcement as did several other of Jean's friends.

WATTS: Go on.

MARLENA: The announcement was relaying the sudden death of Jean in Colorado.

WATTS: Yes, I see. Yes...Ms. Holcomb can you go over your notes again. (Marlena begins retelling the story word for word. Watts is recording the information on a transparency word for word but cannot keep up, and keeps interrupting Marlena to have her repeat details.)

MARLENA: Inspector Watts I have to apologize, the battery on my cell phone is almost dead. I will relay my message as precisely as I can, but you will need to just get the important facts or I am afraid I will lose you. I will make an appointment to meet with you later. (Marlena goes over her story, Watts records only the facts, and then the notes are projected onto the screen for the class to reconstruct the story.)

Handout The Case of the Salty Pickerel

Written by Matthew Harrington

A very rare ruby had recently disappeared from the Glitz and Glitter Jewelry Gallery on the North Beach Boardwalk. A few days later, a jewelry storeowner from the South Beach Boardwalk called the local Chief of Police, Captain Brower, and whispered that a man named Peter Broome was in his store asking many unusual questions about the value of the stolen jewel. When Captain Brower arrived at the jewelry store, Peter admitted that he had the ruby and agreed to go to police headquarters to answer some questions.

"How did you happen to come into possession of this ruby?" asked Captain Brower.

"I found it," answered Broome.

"Hmm," smiled the Captain, "well, today's your lucky day. There's a reward out for the safe return of this ruby."

Broome glanced around nervously, "Really? A reward? Well, gosh! Land sakes alive, can you imagine that. I'll take it, where do I collect?"

"We'll just have to fill out a little paperwork, then you'll be on your way." Captain Brower fumbles in his desk for some papers. "Yes, sir," he smiled. "We depend on good citizens like you to keep our community safe."

"Yes, I know," Broome said cheerily. "In fact, that's how I found the jewel in the first place. You know trying to be a good citizen."

"Oh?" Captain Brower was now uncapping his pen. "Tell me about that."

"Certainly. I was walking along the beach and I looked up in the sky. I saw, I don't know, maybe six, seven, eight seagulls way high up making lazy circles in the air. I thought to myself, I bet someone is hurt and those seagulls are just waiting for them to die so they can have dinner. I better go see if I can help. Well, sir, when I got there, it wasn't anybody hurt at all. It was a huge pickerel that had washed up on shore. I was just about to walk away and go about my business when I saw this shimmering in the pickerel's mouth...and there it was, the ruby that you're holding in your hand right now. Can I have my reward?"

Captain Brower put his pen down and called his assistant, Officer Danno, to come in the room.

"Peter Broome, I'm placing you under arrest for the theft of this ruby! Book him Danno."

How did Captain Brower crack this salty case?

Lesson 3: Becoming a Good Detective

Overview

Analyze. In order to be good detectives, students must learn to be observ**ANT**. Keep a cool head. Think. Ponder. Ask themselves questions. Students must learn strategies for thinking about their topic. Students need to think of what they already know. They need to be taught how to look for keywords and to consider sentence structure to gather basic background information before they can begin to make decisions of what they need or want to know. I call this SIK ("Stuff I Know") and SINK ("Stuff I Need to Know"). I tell them it is pretty SIK if we stay where we are. It is important to turn on the faucet and learn something new (SINK). There are important decisions to be made. There are clues all around. Students must contemplate what they already know before they can proceed. A research statement should be the beginning place to discover clues. Teaching keywords is the springboard for research.

Information Literacy Standards:

Standard 1: Indicators 1, 2, 3, 5
Standard 3: Indicators 1, 2
Standard 6: Indicator 2

★ Objectives:

Students will be able to:

- Recognize keywords in research statements
- Gather clues to find out what they know about their topic
- Ask themselves questions about what they need to know about their topic

Materials:

- PowerPoint presentation or transparencies on being a good detective, this PowerPoint is reinforced in the detective's casebook on pages 68-69
- LCD projector or overhead projector
- Casebooks (Be an LMC Detective, pages 70-71)

⚷⚊ Strategies:

Brainstorm keyword strategies using the slides provided to make your own PowerPoint presentation or to make transparencies. Demonstrate SIK ("Stuff I Know"). What fact statements can the students write about based on the clues in their topic statements or questions? Students will be guided to look at sentence structures and ideas that are provided in their topics.

As you and the students read over the assignment on pages 70-71 in the casebook, have them highlight keywords, circle entire paragraphs, or code information to which they should refer back. Once you have gone over the entire assignment with the students they should write in their own words everything that will be expected for them to complete this project. Knowing what is expected of them and having them write about it will give you a tool for assessing whether they need more clarification. At the same time it will give the students a focus and something to refer back to as they progress through the research assignment.

Modification:

Instead of having the students fill out what is expected on pages 70-71 in the casebook, have them make a bulleted list as you go over the requirements on an overhead or smart board. List should be as follows:

- Complete casebook
- Areas of the library (you can cut this back to the capabilities of the students, and list exactly where you want the citations to come from)
    Reference
    Nonfiction
    Electronic resources
    Print media
- Oral presentation (or you may choose an optional end product)

On the back of this list you may go over the tools the students would use in each of the areas. Once this sheet is finished you might want to laminate it for the students to use as they move from place to place in the library. This tool will remind them of the places they will hunt and what tools in each of the areas will be helpful. It will also be a constant reminder of what is expected for the finished product.

✓ Evaluation:

- Discussion of keywords as clues to beginning research
- Observation of responses to questions that might be posed as you move through the PowerPoint presentation
- Completion and understanding of what is expected as recorded on page 71 in the casebook

Mystery
in the
Media Center

Qualities of a Good Detective

Be observANT:

There are importANT decisions to be made!

- Ask yourself and others questions
- Nothing is something
- Think of all your possibilities

There are importANT decisions to be made!

There are clues all around!

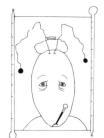

SIK
Stuff I Know

It's pretty sick if we don't learn anything new!

QUESTIONS TO ASK YOURSELF

? WHO IS INVOLVED? (PERSON OR THING)

? WHAT HAS HAPPENED? (EVENT)

? WHERE DID THIS HAPPEN? (PLACE)

? WHEN DID MY EVENT OCCUR? (CURRENT OR LONG AGO)

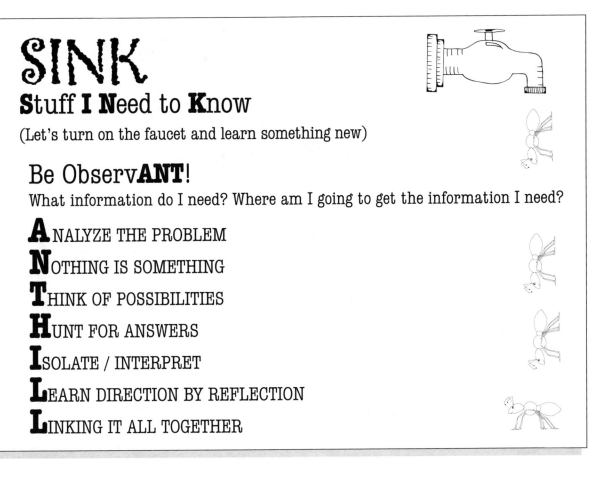

SINK
Stuff I Need to Know
(Let's turn on the faucet and learn something new)

Be ObservANT!
What information do I need? Where am I going to get the information I need?

ANALYZE THE PROBLEM
NOTHING IS SOMETHING
THINK OF POSSIBILITIES
HUNT FOR ANSWERS
ISOLATE / INTERPRET
LEARN DIRECTION BY REFLECTION
LINKING IT ALL TOGETHER

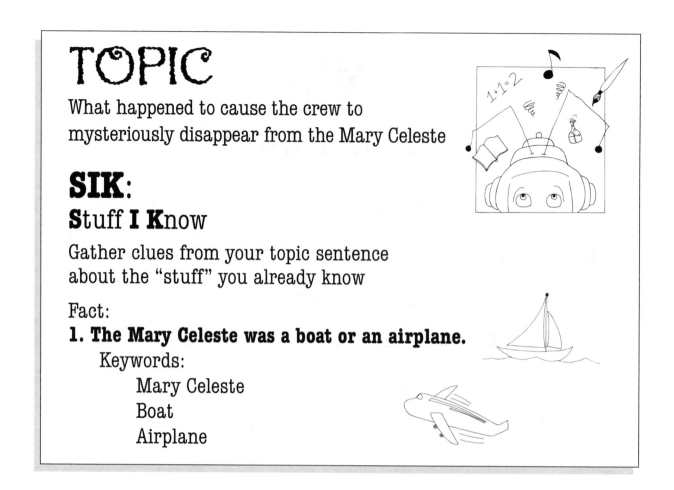

TOPIC

What happened to cause the crew to mysteriously disappear from the Mary Celeste

SIK:

Stuff I Know

Gather clues from your topic sentence about the "stuff" you already know

Fact:

1. The Mary Celeste was a boat or an airplane.

　　Keywords:

　　　　Mary Celeste

　　　　Boat

　　　　Airplane

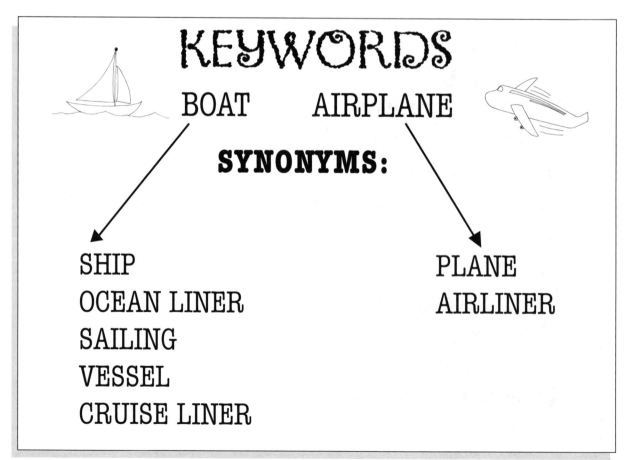

KEYWORDS

BOAT　　AIRPLANE

SYNONYMS:

SHIP

OCEAN LINER

SAILING

VESSEL

CRUISE LINER

PLANE

AIRLINER

SIK
Stuff I Know

FACT:

2. A crew has disappeared.

KEYWORDS:

CREW ──────────────────►

DISAPPEARED ──────────►

SYNONYMS:

STAFF
TEAM
SAILORS

MISSING
VANISHED

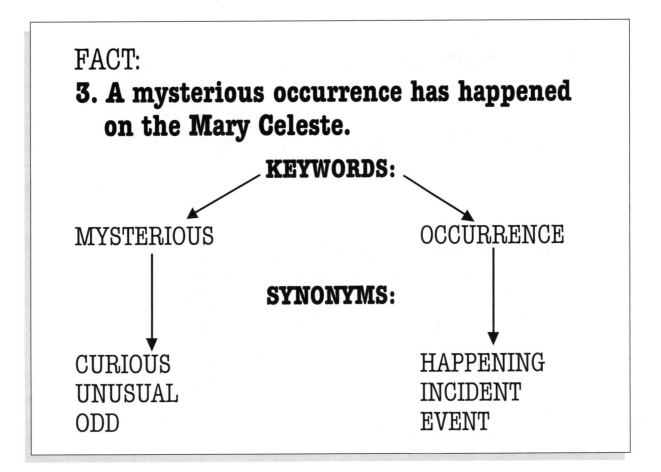

FACT:

3. A mysterious occurrence has happened on the Mary Celeste.

KEYWORDS:

MYSTERIOUS

OCCURRENCE

SYNONYMS:

CURIOUS
UNUSUAL
ODD

HAPPENING
INCIDENT
EVENT

Be an LMC Detective

You are now a Library Media Center (LMC) Crime Solver. During your investigation you will be reporting to Captains _____ and _____ at Information Headquarters. You will be investigating a real life mystery topic. Your investigation will require you to use 5 sources from 4 different areas of the LMC.

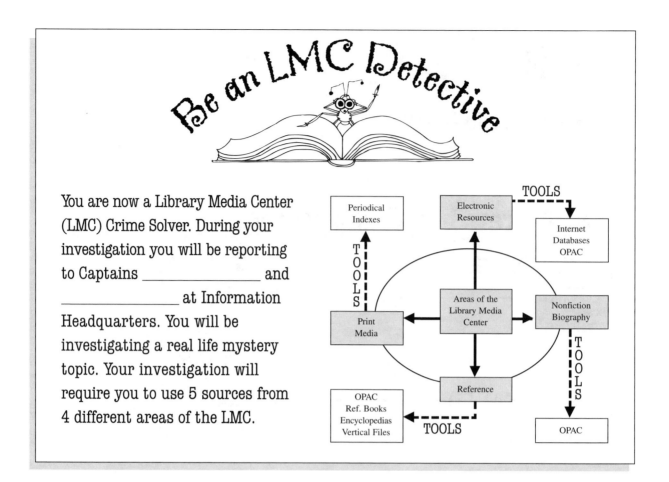

You will complete a bibliography of the sources you use.

You MUST have 5 citations.

Area of the Library Media Center (LMC)	Number of citations needed for your bibliography
Reference	1 citation for your bibliography
Nonfiction / Biography	2 citations for your bibliography, 1 from the Internet and 1 from a database
Electronic Sources	1 citation for your bibliography
Print Media	1 citation for your bibliography

UNDERSTANDING THE CRIME SCENE
Why take notes?

Inside the Crime Scene you will need to make important decisions. There are clues all around you that may be easy to miss unless you know what you are looking for. Your investigations may seem hard at times because the crime scene is so full of information. Before a good detective begins his crime solving process, he stops to think and ponder and absorb all that is around him so as not to miss any important details.

ART of NOTETAKING

Copy

Highlight

Circle

Code

Lesson 4: What Is the Concept?

Overview

What are keywords? What conclusions can be drawn from keywords? What connections can be made? These questions are the beginning of research. Mapping concepts can help define keywords, organize keywords into categories, families, broader and narrower terms, and help students decide in what direction they should launch their search. During this stage students may need to consult dictionaries, biographical dictionaries, and encyclopedias to help them define terms and gather simple background information. Search strategy statements can then be formed based on the terms students have brainstormed. Students will develop "I wonder" statements in the process of guiding them into inquiry research

Information Literacy Standards:

Standard 1: Indicators 1, 2, 3, 5
Standard 3: Indicators 1, 2, 3

★ Objectives:

Students will be able to:

- Recognize the need for task definition before beginning a research project
- Develop information seeking strategies using concept maps
- Identify what they already know about their topic through keywords, narrow and broad topics, and using nothing is something

Materials:

- Casebooks pages 72-73
- Mystery Concept Map Transparency
- Mystery Word (copy word from dictionary). Transparency or you can project the definition from an online dictionary
- Individual Mystery Topics (copied from list included on pages 27-28 of the teacher book or you can develop your own topics based on your unique collection)

🗝 Strategies:

Review "Be an LMC Detective"

Brainstorm the word mystery using a photocopy and transparency of the Mystery Concept Map and a transparency of the word mystery with definitions (a transparency can be made from an online or print dictionary). Demonstrate how to use dictionaries to map the word as you get them started on filling out the page in their casebooks (pages 72-73). Allow time for them to work on their own to finish filling out the map. Follow-up by filling in a mystery word map using an overhead, whiteboard, or a smart board, with the class participating in helping you fill in the map from what they discovered on their own. Assign individual mystery topics. Sample topics are listed in the teacher book on pages 27-28. Copy and cut apart to distribute randomly to the students. The topics presented were developed in collaboration with language arts and with the collection in mind. Topics can be modified for other curricular areas. Unsolved mysteries exist in many disciplines. There are the mysteries of space, the mysteries of history, the mysteries of science and health, and many others. After you have handed out the topics, the students will be excited to share their topics with each other. You might want to take some time and go around the room and have them read their topics out loud. After sharing, have the students circle the keywords in their topic. There are three questions that are listed on each of the topic statements, "What is the event?" "Where did your mystery take place?" and "Who is involved in your mystery (person or thing)?" Have the students try to answer these questions. Not everyone will be able to answer all three questions, but these questions ignite curiosity and help guide the students in their efforts to begin developing their own questions about their mysteries.

Have students refer to casebooks as you go over the entire case assignment, instructing the students to record their name, class, and mystery topic on the cover of their casebook. Assign SIK ("Stuff I Know"), casebook page 72.

SIK=Looking at clues in a topic question or statement, students need to write down statements relating to things they can figure out about their topic before they start researching. This was demonstrated in the PowerPoint from lesson three. If the students were able to answer the three questions on their topic handouts, these answers would be a good starting point for them. Make sure to instruct the students to write in complete sentences and that they should avoid using pronouns in each of their sentences. Using pronouns does not help the students as they begin to think about broad and narrow categories, so steer them away from using it, she, he, they, them, and so on.

Modification:

Work with the classroom teacher to have a lesson and practice about keywords and synonyms before the lesson in the media center. Instead of having students write three sentences about what they already know about their topic, have them make a bulleted list. You might also decide to have students work in pairs on a single topic, if needed.

✓ Evaluation:

- Classroom participation as you review "Be an LMC Detective."

- Successful completion of mystery concept map photocopied from below and classroom participation as you go over mapping the word. You will model the mapping as a follow-up after you have allowed the students to spend time working on their own to complete the map using dictionaries and thesauri for help in completing the map.

- What can the students figure out about their topic just from the clues in the sentences? Students must write three *complete* sentences of something they can figure out about their topic from clues in the topic statements.

- Recognition of keywords. Were the students able to recognize keywords in their topic sentence? Were students able to pick out keywords from their own sentences?

- Completion of keyword list and list of synonyms or other words to use if their keywords do not work. Observe the students' use of dictionaries, encyclopedias, biographical dictionaries, and thesauri as they search for new words.

- Writing in complete sentences (students should not use pronouns).

Figure 5: Mystery Concept Map

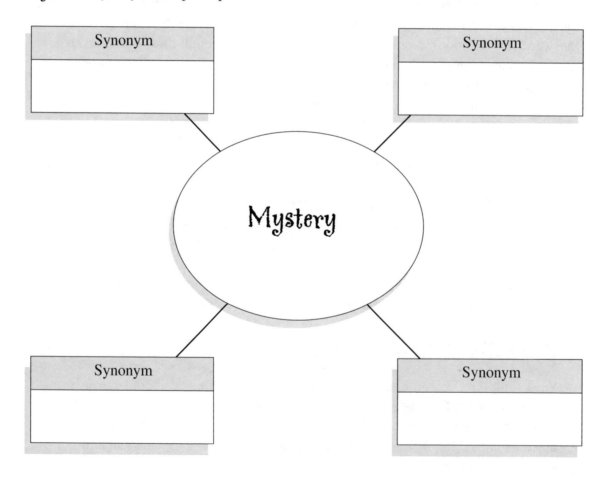

Mystery Topic List

For each mystery topic consider these three questions:

1. What is the event?

2. Where did your mystery take place?

3. Who is involved in your mystery (person or thing)?

- Is it possible that Anastasia Romanov, Russian Princess, is still living? What caused her death?

- The Anasazi Indians, or Cliff Dwellers, disappeared from a place called Mesa Verde, Colorado. What was the cause of their disappearance?

- Will anyone ever know if Lizzie Borden committed the world famous Fall River, Massachusetts murders?

- Why is the disappearance of the people known as the Lost Colony of Roanoke a mystery?

- What are the theories surrounding the assassination of President John F. Kennedy in Dallas, Texas?

- Why is there a mystery surrounding the last flight of Amelia Earhart, which started from Oakland, California?

- What happened to cause the crew to mysteriously disappear from the Mary Celeste?

- What really happened to the crew during World War II Navy testing, in Philadelphia Harbor that has become known as the Philadelphia Experiment or Project Invisibility?

- What is the cause of the appearance of crop circles in various locations across the United States and England?

- Is there a treasure buried on Oak Island, off the coast of Nova Scotia?

- What is the controversy surrounding the untimely death of Marilyn Monroe, glamour girl of Hollywood?

- Could there be a Loch Ness Monster living at the bottom of the dark water lake in Scotland?

- Who built the pyramids of Ancient Egypt?

- Did aliens really land in Roswell, New Mexico in what has become known as the Roswell incident?

- Why is the disappearance of Agatha Christie, famous English novelist, such a mystery?

- What caused the dinosaurs to disappear from the earth?

- Was there ever a city called Atlantis, and if there was, what caused it to vanish?

- What is the conspiracy surrounding the assassination of President Abraham Lincoln, at Ford's Theatre?

- What is mysterious about the deaths of 12-year-old Crown Prince Edward V of England and his younger brother Richard, who mysteriously disappeared during the Hundred Years War?

- What are the unanswered questions surrounding the assassination of Malcolm X in Manhattan, New York?

- What are the various theories surrounding the mysterious death of Wolfgang Amadeus Mozart, a great European composer?

- Where or how did the Moai, or stone giants, that stand on Easter Island come to be there?

- How or why did the large stones standing at Stonehenge come to be there?

- What has supposedly caused ships and planes to vanish in the Bermuda Triangle?

- Is there really a Yeti (or Abominable Snowman), sometimes also known as Bigfoot, living in various locations around the world?

- Did Betty and Barney Hill really get abducted by aliens aboard an unidentified flying object?

- Was Napoleon Bonaparte, Emperor of France, murdered or could he have died of natural causes?

- What is the mystery surrounding the crystal skull discovered by Anna Mitchell Hedges in a Mayan village in Mexico?

Lesson 5: It is No Beef, Just Boolean

Overview

Understanding the use of synonyms and the ability to construct concept maps will provide quick engagement with information. Once these problem-solving skills are put into action, the students will need to begin linking concepts together and formulating search statements.

Information Literacy Standards:

Standard 1: Indicators 1, 2, 3, 4, 5
Standard 3: Indicators 2
Standard 6: Indicators 2

★ Objectives:

Students will be able to:

- Understand use of synonyms when constructing concept maps
- Understand the need to gather quick information from dictionaries and encyclopedias in order to begin research
- Gather keywords and begin building search strategies that will include Boolean logic and phrase searching

Materials:

- Case books
- Transparencies
    Mystery Concept Map for review (see Lesson 4)
    Topic Concept Map for brainstorming their own mysteries
    Boolean logic
    Pyramid transparency
- Transparency markers
- Overhead projector
- LCD Projector (to demonstrate search strategies)
- Computer

Strategies:

Collect and review mystery concept maps photocopied from page 26.

Assign topic concept maps found in casebook on page 74. Have students write their entire topic, word for word, in the circle in the center of the Topic Concept Map. Allow time for them to map their topic, recording the event, location, person, or thing. Under person or thing they will be encouraged to access dictionaries, biographical dictionaries, and encyclopedias to help them with the "nothing is something" concept.

Assign Broad to Narrow Topic: Building the Pyramid page 75. Help the students as they build their pyramids. Some pyramids can be built all the way to the top and others can only be built one or two levels. Working from the top of the pyramid down, an example would be: Mary Celeste, Mystery Ship, Famous Ship, Ships. Or, another example might be: Abraham Lincoln, Assassinated President, United States President, World Leader.

Figure 6: Pyramid Example

Demonstrate using an encyclopedia to build the pyramid. Start the discussion by asking the students where they might find information about Mary Celeste in an encyclopedia. Some will say the M volume, some will say the C volume. Pull the M volume and demonstrate. Pull the C volume and demonstrate. Some students might say the S volume, pull that volume and demonstrate. After modeling these different ways of looking, pull the index volume and show how easy it is to find an entry for Mary Celeste if using the index volume first. If you don't find Mary Celeste try another encyclopedia set. This is a good demonstration as well to show students that every encyclopedia set is different, that research is not easy, and if you don't find your topic in the first thing you pick up, try, try again. Once you have found Mary Celeste you can demonstrate building the pyramid using this topic.

Figure 6: Pyramid Example

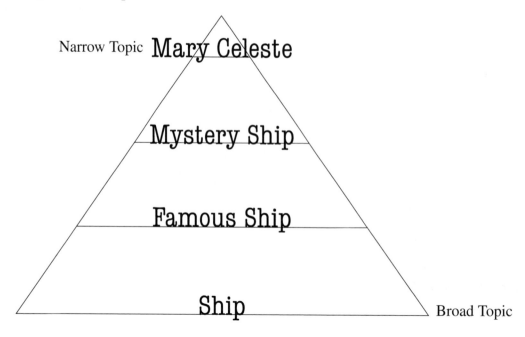

Narrow Topic **Mary Celeste**

Mystery Ship

Famous Ship

Ship Broad Topic

Nothing Is Something

When the answers are not obvious students must be guided to look at the problem from a different angle. They must be guided to consider options when gathering information or forming search strategies. "Nothing is something" is the time to stop, to look at the problem in a different way, to rethink, and to discover new ways around any obstacles that are experienced. I tell my students a story about doing research for a college term paper on the topic of cancer. The student doing research went into a medical library and found there were no entries in the OPAC for cancer. What to do? How could that be possible, especially in a medical library? I help the students discover that when a dead end occurs (as seems to happen while doing research), that "nothing" creates opportunity for discovery, leading to something else, a new definition, and a new way of looking at an old problem. When the student doing research on cancer found out that the medical library terms "cancer" as "neoplasm," the quest for answers to the research on cancer is able to be tackled. Students begin to understand that when a term, keyword, or search strategy is not working they can think of synonyms, narrow categories, broad topics, or other ways to solve their problem.

Review use of encyclopedias, dictionaries, and biographical dictionaries for use in beginning research.

Provide instruction in use of keywords, synonyms, and search strategies for use with electronic information resources and for knowledge acquisition of their assigned topic using Boolean logic and phrase searching. Use Boolean logic transparency for demonstration purposes. You can demonstrate the use of Boolean logic by having the students stand up and then taking a count as indicated on the transparency. By actually having students stand up, they will see the numbers change according to the linker (and, or, or not) that is being demonstrated.

Modification:

To teach broad and narrow categories you might use the following example: Linda has on a red shirt, Jennifer has on a blue sweater, Joe has on a black hoody, I have on a pink jacket. What category or family do all of these items belong to? (Answer should be clothes.) Once you have that answer you can help the students think of other words to use for clothes, apparel, or fashion. You can also use this demonstration to show the large category to the narrow: Clothing, Tops, Shirt, Red Shirt.

✓ Evaluation:

- Observations of students' ability to contribute during class discussion as you go over the mystery concept map, their topic concept maps, and their interaction during Boolean logic demonstration.
- Completion of Topic Concept Map on page 74 in the casebook.
- Completion of Pyramid on page 75 in the casebook.

As the students are filling in the concept map and the pyramid, you should observe whether they are using resource materials in their attempt to complete these pages. You may need to guide them to the tools that will be helpful, such as, dictionaries, encyclopedias (using the index volume), special encyclopedias, and biographical tools.

Figure 7: Topic Concept Map

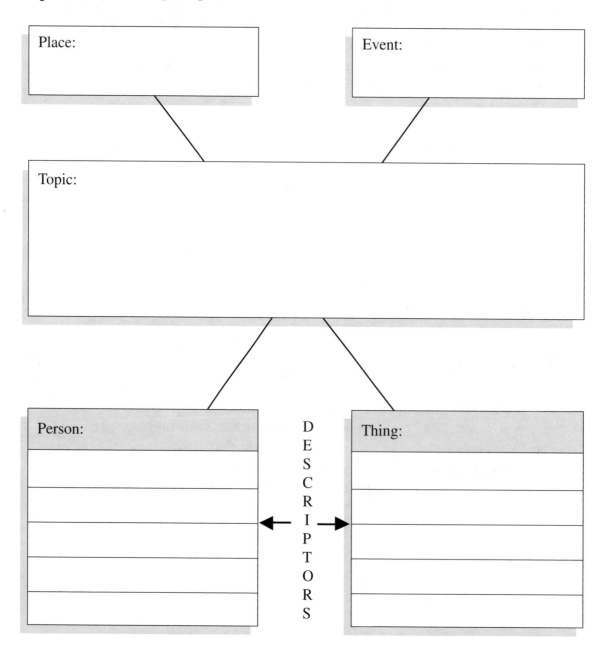

Figure 8: Pyramid

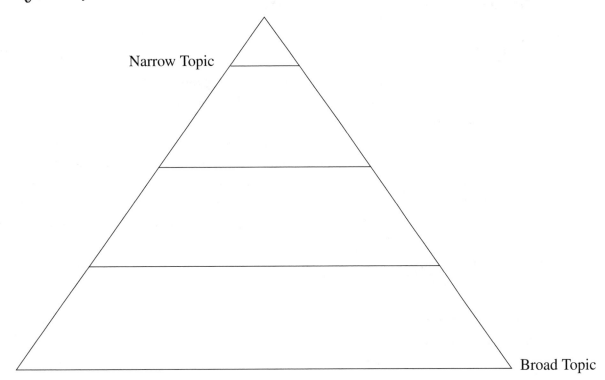

Narrow Topic

Broad Topic

Figure 9: Boolean Logic

Blue Jean AND Sweatshirt

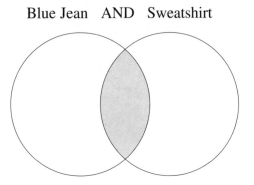

Diagram for Boolean Operator "AND"

Blue Jean OR Sweatshirt

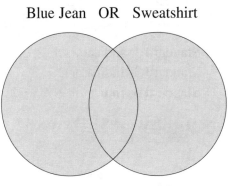

Diagram for Boolean Operator "OR"

Blue Jean NOT Sweatshirt

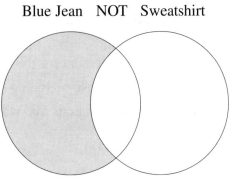

Diagram for Boolean Operator "NOT"

Lesson 6: Making Your Statement

Overview

It is important that students learn to ask crime scene questions: "What will I use to help me locate information?" "What areas of the crime scene must I investigate?" "Once I find the tools, how will I find information in those tools?" "What will my final product be?" "How will I get there?" Students should express what they want to learn through "I Wonder" statements. Students also need to take a look at their feelings about their assignment. Getting started on a research project is usually the point where students are most confused and anxious about what they really need to get accomplished, where to start, and what is required. Recording their feelings and stating their course of action will help them begin to take ownership of their project, and hopefully ignite interest in their topic. Dr. Kuhlthau has done extensive research arguing that information professionals need to be aware of the stages of feelings that their information seekers are experiencing in their quest for meaning. By understanding these feelings, the professional can intervene and provide guidance.

Information Literacy Standards:

Standard 1: Indicators 1, 2, 3, 4, 5
Standard 3: Indicator 2
Standard 6: Indicator 2

★ Objectives:

Students will be able to:

- Identify what is needed to complete this project (keeping focus is important when doing any research)
- Record their beginning anxieties and/or excitement for the research process
- Construct keyword search strategies using phrase searching and Boolean logic
- Think creatively about their topics and ask questions that will help direct their search process

Materials:

- Casebooks pages 76, 77
- Search strategy plan "Making Your Statement" in student casebook, page 85
- Computers
- LCD projector

Strategies:

Guide students to discover what they want to find out about their topic. Students should record, in their casebooks, as many "I Wonder" statements as they can think of. This will help them form search strategies that will keep them focused on their topic as they hunt for answers. You will want to model writing essential questions for the students, so that they can use that model to form their own statements. Writing essential questions takes practice. For some great examples on developing essential questions you might want to look at Biopoint on the Internet <http://www.biopoint.com>. Some of the students' "I Wonder" statements will be fact gathering questions, as they need to be, but they should develop at least one essential question about their topic that will lead them to make some sort of conclusion or opinion about their topic. An example of an essential question about the Mary Celeste might be: If the crew disappeared because of a storm or natural cause, could they have prepared themselves for this kind of danger? Most likely the students will be excited about their topics, but some may feel fearful that they will not be able to find anything. They have grown up with the Internet and in most cases that is where they will want to begin their search because students generally believe that the Internet is the place where they can find anything. The "I Wonder" statements will be the anchor that will draw the students back to the information they are seeking. The overwhelming amount of information that is available to students can create a high level of frustration and retrieval of relevant information is many times illusive if they are not taught how to think about what they are looking for in the first place. Attention to keywords and alternative words to use to string together in a way that will produce the results they want is critical to helping them overcome these feelings.

Demonstrate search strategies using keywords, Boolean logic, and phrase searching on the Internet. First demonstrate searching without quotations. Draw students' attention to the number of search results. Now form good search statements using quotation marks and using Boolean logic. Students will see the importance of good search strategies to get the results they want. Demonstrate these same strategies for databases.

Instruct students to search their topics and record their results in their casebooks.

Modification:

Have students work on search statements before they go to the computers. You might use different colored paper for students' search terms write phrase-searched words together on the same piece of paper, and write other keywords on separate pieces of paper. This really turns out to be a manipulative graphic organizer.

✓ Evaluation:

- Completion of "I Wonder" statements in their casebooks on page 76, including one essential question

- Observation of students as they conduct their searches using the Internet and databases

- Observation of students as they put together search strategies and work through "Making Your Statement" found on page 85 of their casebooks

- Completion of Making Your Statement on page 85 of their casebook: What search strategies did they use? Did they use quotations and Boolean logic correctly?

- Printout on their topic from the Internet and implementation of highlighting techniques. Students need to read their printout and highlight, circle, and code. They should find words in the document that they have not thought of before and record those new words in the grid provided on page 85 of their casebook. This should be repeated for the database. By completion of this lesson the students should have two printouts, one from the Internet and one from a database, and each should have keywords highlighted.

Lesson 7: Amazing Tools

Overview

It is now time to investigate the crime scene. Location and access is the name of the game as the detectives begin implementing the tools of the trade and hunt for answers.

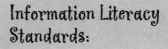

Information Literacy Standards:

Standard 1: Indicators 1, 2, 3, 4, 5
Standard 3: Indicator 2
Standard 6: Indicator 2

★ Objectives:

Students will be able to:

- Focus on what is needed to complete their investigation
- Identify four areas of the library and the tools (resources) they will use to do their research
- Assess how their case is progressing

Materials:

- Casebooks
- Hunt for Answers, Summarizing, Isolate/Interpret

⌐ Strategies:

Introduce and assign "Hunting for Answers" (Scene of the Crime Sheets) from the casebooks.

Explain to the students that they will need to record their search strategies. What worked, what did not work? What keywords or search strategies did they use in the OPAC, encyclopedia indexes, and periodical indexes? Once the students have found good information about their topic, they will need to make a copy of their chapter, article, or pertinent information and read, highlight, circle, and code important facts and ideas. They should record their findings by filling out the summarizing pages and the Isolate/Interpret pages for each of the resource materials from which they gather information. The Isolate/Interpret pages are a chance for the students to reflect back on their "I wonder" statements in order to make sure that they are staying focused on their information gathering. This portion of the project will run over several days with students accessing information from the various resource material located in the different areas of the library. Areas of the library media center they will gather their information from are: Reference, Nonfiction, Print, and Electronic Media. After a couple of days have the students stop to reflect on their process. Teach Lesson Eight and then return to Hunting for Answers.

Modification:

Reduce the number of citations. Remind students that when they are working on the Isolate/Interpret pages that they must look back at the "I Wonder" statements. The "I Wonder" page is indicated with an *eye* in the upper right hand corner.

✔ Evaluation:

Observation of students as they search in all areas of the media center: Are the students using the index volumes? What keywords are they using? Are they finding new keywords? What kind of search strategies are they implementing? Are they using Boolean logic and phrase searching as they go to the Internet and databases? Once they have found their information are they reading, highlighting, and journaling about the source material on the appropriate pages? Are they referring back to their "I Wonder" statements for each of the sources to make sure they are answering their research questions?

Students' understanding and completion of assigned casebook pages (Scene of the Crime Log Sheets and Summary Sheets for each source. Isolate/Interpret Sheets.) Use Assessment tools provided.

Figure 10: Ref Non Fic Assessment

Checklist for Assessing
Scene of the Crime Log Sheets

REFERENCE AND NONFICTION

REFERENCE and NONFICTION SOURCES	Complete	Incomplete	Partially
Keyword list			
Encyclopedia: keyword listed			
Bibliographic citation			
Book: OPAC search shown			
Call number recorded			
Photocopy of source material			
Source material highlighted			
Summary			
Main idea is listed			
Three supporting details are recorded			
New keywords recorded			

Checklist for Assessing Scene of the Crime Log Sheets

ELECTRONIC RESOURCES
INTERNET/DATABASE

ELECTRONIC SOURCES	Complete	Incomplete	Partially
Keyword list			
Search Strategy keyword listed			
Recorded results citation			
Database/search engine listed			
Bibliographic citation			
Printout of source material			
Source material highlighted			
Summary			
Main idea is listed			
Three supporting details are recorded			
New keywords recorded			

Figure 12: Print Media Assessment

Checklist for Assessing
Scene of the Crime Log Sheets

PRINT MEDIA

PRINT MEDIA SOURCES	Complete	Incomplete	Partially
Keyword list			
Index listed			
Bibliographic citation			
If article not found on shelf did students go to a database to find article?			
Photocopy of source material			
Source material highlighted			
Summary			
Main idea is listed			
Three supporting details are recorded			
New keywords recorded			

Lesson 8: Direction by Reflection

Overview

A detective's work is difficult at times. There are so many clues and important decisions to be made. A good detective has to know how to stop, ponder, and absorb the vast amount of information available. Rethinking is a necessary task a good detective must learn. When stumped, when it seems the detective has run out of options, when the detective hits that "nothing" spot in research, the detective must remember that "nothing is something." This realization will enable the good detective to proceed in a different direction.

Information Literacy Standards:

Standard 1: Indicators 2, 3, 4, 5
Standard 2: Indicators 1, 2, 3, 4
Standard 3: Indicator 1
Standard 5: Indicator 5
Standard 6: Indicator 6
Standard 7: Indicators 1, 2

 Objectives:

Students will be able to:

- Identify four different areas of the Media Center
- Understand searching strategies while using the traditional card catalog, OPAC, and Electronic Resources (Internet and databases)
- Understand nothing is something in order to change direction or strategies, if necessary
- Locate and access resources in all areas of the media center (reference materials, magazine indexes, Internet, CD-ROMs, nonfiction, or biography collection)
- Take notes on accessed material
- Reflect about their ways of searching

Materials:

- Casebook, page 96

  Learn from your mistakes (Direction by Reflection)

⚷ Strategies:

Review "Nothing is something" and have students reflect on what they have accomplished up to this point in their research. Have them examine the keywords they have been using. Have those words worked? Should they try something else? What has been hard about their topic and/or research? What new things have they learned about their topic and themselves as a researcher?

Review the scene of the crime sheets that have been completed up to this point.

Explain and assign Direction by Reflection found on page 96.

Direction by Reflection is the point in research where students are guided to reflect on what strategies have worked, what have not, what has been learned about search strategies, things to do differently, and whether there are gaps in understanding. This is approximately mid-point in the project and students should do some self-assessment. They need to reflect on where they started and if the strategies they are using are moving them toward their end result. The students will then return to their research process, thinking about the strategies that have worked or not and perhaps even shifting gears to head in a different direction.

✓ Evaluation:

- Completion of Search Strategy Plan
- Participation in discussion of Scene of the Crime Sheets
- Observation of search strategies using OPAC, card catalog, Internet, and databases

Students should be allowed time to journal about their hunt for information. This writing can be done in the classroom. This is like a journal entry page and should not be graded except for noting if it is done or not done. This page is a good way for students to think about what works for them and to talk about it. The journaling will also help you to understand the students' strategies and offer insight for intervention where needed.

Lesson 9: Giving Credit Where Credit Is Due

Overview

When researchers pick up a piece of written work, they should be able to discover where the ideas used in the work came from. Students must learn that if they are going to be responsible members of any academic community they must give credit where credit is due. When using the language or ideas of someone else, the researcher must refer the reader to the originating source by supplying a bibliographic citation. Throughout this guided research process, there has been ample opportunity for the students to record their findings by asking them specific questions about the information they have retrieved. A copy of each of their source materials must be turned in, and each copy must show how they implemented the highlighting strategy. The casebooks ask guiding questions that make the students think about and respond to what they have read and highlighted in each of their source materials. Students must be taught about plagiarism, it is not enough to give stern warnings about plagiarizing. By guiding the students in highlighting strategies and the writing process, where you are conferencing with them at each juncture, you are guiding them to form their own opinions that lead them away from plagiarizing. While the Internet has provided an easy opportunity for cutting and pasting, it is also a place where plagiarism can easily be caught. Plagiarizing is not just a cut and paste issue; it is an issue of ideas. Just like I can own a book, I can own ideas. If someone takes my book without asking permission that is called stealing. If someone takes an idea without asking permission that, too, is stealing. If someone wants to borrow my book, and asks, and I grant permission that is okay, but what if I have given permission for someone to borrow my book and they go around telling everyone it is their book. Is that okay? That, too, is stealing. There are several wonderful resources and lesson plans available on the Internet to teach about plagiarism. Doing a search on "lesson plans" *and* plagiarism will give many great lessons to infuse here as you teach the students how to pull together their citations into a bibliography. You will find a list of plagiarism Web sites listed in the Recommended Reading List on page 99.

Information Literacy Standards:

Standard 8: Indicators 1, 2

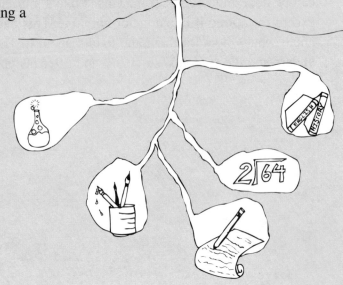

★ Objectives:

Students will be able to:

- Gain knowledge of the construction of bibliographic citation
- Demonstrate competency to locate, access, and compile information from several different types of library sources in order to create a bibliography
- Understand citation construction based on differing sources
- Construct their bibliography from the citation templates found in their Scene of the Crime Log Sheets

Materials:

- Citation information from casebooks
- Blank transparency, white board, smart board, or computer
- Overhead projector or LCD projector
- Internet connection to demonstrate Noodletools if you have a subscription (There are other Web sites to help with bibliographic citation that you can find in the recommended reading section of this book.)

⚷ Strategies:

Introduce the construction of bibliographic citation. Demonstrate, for the students, how to take information from the templates recorded in their casebook Scene of the Crime Log Sheets and put it into bibliographic format. Use a single citation and put it together on a transparency and project it with an overhead projector or type the information into a word document using an LCD projector to project what you are doing. You may also use a white board or smart board. If you have Noodletools (this is a wonderful subscription-required tool for building bibliographies that can be found online at <www.noodletools.com>), you can demo how to use it to the class using an LCD projector connected to your computer. If you do not have means to access Noodletools, the students can compile their bibliographies based on the templates in their casebooks or examples from the Noodletools Web site. There are several other Web sites that can help students understand bibliographic construction as well. What is important at this point is helping the students pull together the information they have gathered from the different sources, examine the various theories, and begin formulating their own opinions. Again the use of unsolved mysteries forces the researcher to examine a variety of theories to come to some conclusions as to what they think they would most agree with and why. Students are guided to web their topic and then develop an outline from that web. At this point they should be ready to put together note cards that they will use for their oral presentation. Their finished bibliography must be turned in along with their source materials, the web construction, outline, and note cards.

✓ Evaluation:

- The students will become "expert" in constructing a bibliography for their research
- Completed and correct bibliographic format in alphabetic order
- Completion of web of their topic
- Outline developed from the web

Figure 13: Theories Web

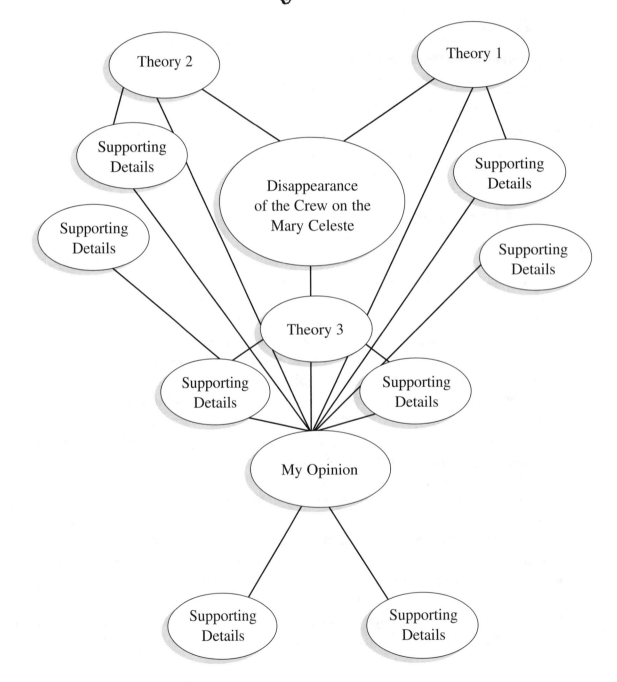

Webbing Your Theories

Lesson 10: Untangling the Web

Overview

Who? When? True? False? When choosing the Internet to do research, the burden is on the researcher to establish the validity, authorship, timeliness, and integrity of what they find. Documents can easily be copied and falsified. In general the World Wide Web has no editors that require certain standards like most print publications. Most pages for the Web are self-published or published by businesses with motives to get you to buy something or believe in their point of view. Even university and library Web sites may have pages that the institution does not oversee. Students need to cultivate the habit of healthy skepticism. They need to question everything they find with critical thinking.

Information Literacy Standards:

Standard 7: Indicators 1, 2
Standard 8: Indicators 1, 2

★ Objectives:

Students will be able to:

- Gain knowledge of the construction of an Internet Web site
- Evaluate an Internet Web site

Materials:

- Internet
- LCD Projector
- Web Evaluation Worksheets, page 92
- Overhead projector
- Transparency: Web Evaluation

🔑 Strategies:

Introduce the construction of Internet Web sites. Students need to learn to identify something about a Web page just by looking at the address. Teach students what they are really searching when they search the Web. Searching the Web is almost like searching through a file cabinet with several drawers. You might open one drawer and inside that drawer is a folder and in that folder are several documents. This is a good illustration that students at this age can understand. Showing students how to deconstruct a Web site helps them become more critical about the information they are accessing. What is the anatomy of a URL (Uniform Resource Locator)?

Breaking Down a URL
URL: http://www.lib.berkeley.edu/TeachingLib/Guides/Internet/Evaluate.html
Type of file (hypertext marc up): http://
Domain (computer file and location on the Internet): www.lib.berkeley.edu
edu = education, gov = government, com = commercial, org = organization
Path or directory on the computer to the file you are accessing:
/TeachingLib/Guides/Internet
Name of file and its file extension (usually ends in .htm or .html): /Evaluate.html
Some good sites to refer to:

Kathy Schrock's Guide for Educators
http://school.discovery.com/schrockguide/eval.html

Evaluating Web Pages: Techniques to Apply & Questions to Ask
http://www.lib.berkeley.edu/TeachingLib/Guides/Internet/Evaluate.html

WWW CyberGuides
http://www.cyberbee.com/guides.html

Go over worksheet with students. See Casebook, page 92
Review plagiarism

✔ Evaluation:

The students will become "expert" in deconstructing an Internet Web site. The students will use the Web evaluation worksheet found in their casebooks on page 92 to evaluate the Web site they use for their research project.

Lesson 11: Linking It All Together

Overview

Thinking about what has been learned and what to do with what has been learned is Direction by Reflection. It is important to think about where the project started, what processes have worked, what knowledge has been gained about the research topic, and to reflect about ways of thinking about doing research. Take everything that has been learned from all the different sources and build new knowledge.

Information Literacy Standards:

Standard 6: Indicators 1, 2

★ Objectives:

Students will be able to:

- Think about what they have learned
- Self evaluate their research process using the worksheets from their casebooks listed below
- Tie together their information to develop opinions and final presentations

Materials:

- Casebooks
    Direction by Reflection, page 96
    Linking It All Together, page 97
    What I Learned, page 98
- Posttest (This will be exactly the same test that was given as the pretest. Every student will receive the same test.)

⊶ Strategies:

Provide time for students to reflect on their research process.

Administer the posttest (Because this test is exactly the same as the pretest it will be a good indicator of knowledge acquisition over the course of the project. I have used this test at other times during the year as a way of tracking retention.)

Modification:

You might need to guide the students to give their topic a title. Once they have a title, you will want to have them make a bulleted list of the things they know about their topic now, what was the easiest thing about doing this project, and what was the hardest thing about doing this project.

✔ Evaluation:

- Observation and examination of student reflections
- Posttest (from Teacher Book page 8-9 Pretest/posttest)

Lesson 12: And Now Presenting

Overview

Now the time has come when the research is over and the presentation begins. Students need to feel comfortable in front of an audience. Learning presentation dynamics and use of visual aids will allow the students to speak about their mystery in a variety of formats (all of which can be video taped and sent to the local television network).

Information Literacy Standards:

Standard 5: Indicators 2, 3
Standard 9: Indicators 1, 2, 3, 4

Objectives:

Students will be able to:

- Give a three-minute oral presentation using only note cards and visual aids
- Evaluate (self and others) presentation dynamics (use of voice, body, eye contact, research content, etc.), using the Speaker's Rubric found at the end of this lesson

Materials:

- Video camera/Video tape
- Microphone/Speakers
- Oral Speaking Rubric in Casebook, page 56
- Speaker's Rubric (If you film the presentations you may want to duplicate this page and have students score each other as they watch the film. They will be able to see themselves and score themselves as well as their peers), page 57
- Background sets, as needed (students can make and bring in)

- Handouts for public speaking strategies in Teacher Book at the end of this lesson
- Evaluating the Casebook Rubric, page 58
- Certificates in Teacher Book at the end of this lesson

⚷ Strategies:

Introduce public speaking by demonstration. If possible invite the high school public speaking class in to demonstrate how to give a good speech. These students will be able to address good posture, vocal quality, good eye contact, and the use of visual aids. They can also model the need for having a good opening, a good body of information, and how to use transition phrases to move through their presentation, and finally, the importance of having a good conclusion. By demonstrating by example a good speech versus a bad speech, the middle school students see the importance of body language, good eye contact, physical appearance, and organized concise content in order to have a quality presentation. Collaborating with the high school provides an opportunity for the high school students to present what they have learned and to model for the middle school students how effective they can be if they are organized (an important middle school lesson).

If you do not have an opportunity for this kind of collaboration Steve Otfinoski's book *Speaking Up, Speaking Out: A Kid's Guide to Making Speeches, Oral Reports, and Conversation* (Millbrook Press, 1996) is perfect for this age group.

Work with students in groups and individually as needed for speech preparation. Students should prepare an outline from the information they have documented in their casebooks. This outline will provide them with the necessary clues to present their information without reading. The classroom teacher might decide to have the students write an essay from their outlines, as well as give an oral presentation. The outline will serve for either purpose. Students will create cue cards for their oral presentation from their outline. A basic outline format is provided at the end of this lesson that you may use to handout to the students or make a transparency to model outlining. Other places to go for outlines, rubrics, and graphic organizers can be found in the recommended reading section of this book. These resources will be helpful if you are using a smart board.

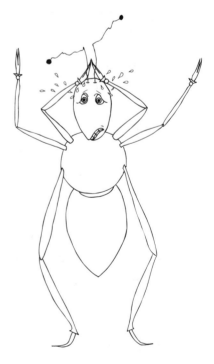

For the oral presentation students may choose to work in groups to present their research. Students may choose to present as if they are a news team on location or as an "unsolved mystery" television show. It is important that each student in a group contribute his or her own three minutes of information, so if there are four people in the group the presentation would be 12 minutes long with each member contributing three minutes. If you decide to film the students' presentations you may choose to have them view each others presentations and use the speaker's rubric for them to anonymously rate each others' oral speaking.

Modification:

You may reduce the time for speaking or you may choose to have students create a visual representation of their topic and explain it.

✔ Evaluation:

Each (group or alone) student will give a three-minute oral presentation, and the teacher will use the Oral Speaking Rubric for evaluating the oral presentation. Even though the students may be working together at this point, you will still want to evaluate each student individually. You will be looking for good eye contact, vocal quality, body language, use of note cards, and content of the speech. It is important that the students have a good introduction and conclusion and that their body of work is supported by details. Also look for use of good transition words such as therefore, however, and in conclusion, to move from one point to another. The rubric includes a place for recording the time limit. You may choose to reinforce time limits by marking down if the time limit requirement is not met.

If you film the presentations you may want the students to evaluate each other using the Speaker's Rubric as they view the presentations. Make sure students score each other anonymously so that students know that they can be absolutely honest. When you allow students to score the presentations in this manner it reinforces the aspects of oral presentation for each student.

Example of Student Outline

Topic: Why do treasure hunters keep digging up Oak Island, a small island off the coast of Nova Scotia?

Title: (from casebook page *)**
Oak Island: The Digging Still Continues

Outline:

I. The digging begins
    A. Daniel McGinnis (1795)
        1. Finds branch that looks like pulley
        2. Finds depression on the ground
    B. 200 years of digging
        1. Still find nothing
    C. Pirates
        1. Tales of buried treasure
II. Body of evidence
    A. Discoveries
        1. Dan brings friends
        2. Flagstone at 2 ft
        3. Layer of oak logs at 10 ft
        4. Other materials
        5. Every 10 ft found oak logs
    B. 8 years later
        1. Onslow company digs
        2. Truro company digs
        3. Blankenship company digs
        4. Charcoal at 40 ft
        5. Layer of putty at 50 ft
    C. Interesting discoveries
        1. Stone at 90 ft water begins seeping into pit
        2. A trap?
        3. Unplugged at 500 ft waterway, water coming from Smith's Cove
III. Conclusion
    A. I believe there is buried treasure
        1. So many people digging
        2. Evidence of man-made structure
        3. Tales of pirates

Figure 15: Example of Sample Notecard

Sample Note Cards for Oral Presentation (Each card should be numbered to keep them in order and students may want to write out their introduction and their conclusion especially if they are quoting. Students will probably have a minimum of three cards: Introduction, Body, and Conclusion. The cards for the body may need more than one card to cover their topic and present all their theories.)

A. Introduction   1

1. The digging begins

    a. Daniel McGinnis (1795)

    b. 200 years of digging

    c. Why they dig—Tales of pirates and buried treasure

A. Body of Evidence   2

1. Discoveries
    a. Flagstone 2 ft
    b. Layer of oak logs every 10 ft
    c. Companies digging
       i. Onslow, Truro, Blankenship
    d. Interesting discoveries
       i. Stone 90 ft and water seeping
       ii. Smith's Cove

Oral Speaking Rubric

Speaker:_____ Record time here:_____

	1 Incomplete	2 Poor	3 Fair	4 Good	5 Excellent
Eye contact Looks at audience, is not reading from cards					
Use of voice Speaks loudly and clearly					
Body language Doesn't swing and sway, good posture					
Use of visuals/audio Refers to visual: visual is well-organized and large enough for audience to see, student may use PowerPoint, video, or other for visual					
Content Good opening					
Content Body: presents details and provides examples, good use of transition words					
Content Good closing: formulates a conclusion with supporting reasons					

Speaker Rubric

Speaker:_____ 1=Poor 5=Excellent Record time here:_____

	1	2	3	4	5
Eye contact					
Use of voice					
Body language					
Use of visuals/audio					

Speaker:_____ 1=Poor 5=Excellent Record time here:_____

	1	2	3	4	5
Eye contact					
Use of voice					
Body language					
Use of visuals/audio					

Speaker:_____ 1=Poor 5=Excellent Record time here:_____

	1	2	3	4	5
Eye contact					
Use of voice					
Body language					
Use of visuals/audio					

Evaluating the Casebook Rubric

	1 Incomplete	2 Poor	3 Fair	4 Good	5 Excellent
Analyzing Understands what is needed to be a good detective and what is needed to do a good job on this project.					
Nothing is something Selects relevant search terms and good keywords. Thinks of broad and narrow topics.					
Think of possibilities Formulates clear "I Wonder" statements that lead to discovery.					
Hunt for answers Use of materials. Relevant sources for information needed. Understands the main idea and supporting details from the material.					
Isolate/Interpret Reflects on "I Wonder" statements. Makes sure that the material gathered answers the questions posed.					
Learn direction by reflection Forms statements about what worked and what hasn't worked at this point in the research.					
Link it all together Reorganizes information, translates findings, and formulates a conclusion. Presentation of research. Bibliographic citation.					
Subtotal					
Total					

Unit Evaluation

Name:	
Topic:	
FINAL GRADE	
Casebook	
Outline	
Note Cards	
Bibliography	
Oral Presentation ■ Use of cue cards _____ (GR) ■ Use of visual _____ (GR) ■ Presentation (3 minutes): Look at oral speaking rubric _____ (GR)	

Wrap Up:

It is now time to celebrate. Once the students have given their presentations, which could be filmed and submitted to your local TV channel, consider having a party that includes a promotion ceremony. During the ceremony promote students from detective to lieutenant inspector and give them a certificate (located at the end of the handouts in this section). If possible, add pictures of the students to the certificates. Once the presentations are finished and the promotion ceremony is over, students may check out mystery novels to read for pleasure.

This unit has focused on unsolved mysteries in collaboration with language arts, but it is important to understand that unsolved mysteries are the hook to get the students excited about doing research. This process can be adapted to any curriculum area, and the ANTHILL is a great way of reminding students to think about their own thinking and approach to information seeking. Once the students have learned this process they can be in for another project and you can say, "remember the pyramid" and they will be reminded to think of broad and narrow topics. I also use a one sheet search page that helps remind students of the process when they come to the media center for short, quick information about any topic. A couple different work sheets you might use are on the next two pages.

Smart Start
Research Planning Worksheet

Building Research Skills By Being ObservANT

A=Analyze the problem, **N**=Nothing is something, **T**=Think of all your possibilities

---

Write a sentence describing what you would like to research:

Look at your sentence from above and circle your keywords then write them in the space below.

Broad and narrow categories

                                 Narrow Topic

                                 Broad Topic

(What if the keywords you have listed don't work? What other words will help you?)
Make a list of any other words that you might use to look for information about your topic.

Do any of the words belong in phrases or strings? (together in a certain order?)
(Search these words using quotes around them like this: "phrase search".) **Show me:**

Draw a Boolean logic map(s) of the keywords that you will use to do an electronic search on your topic. (Use AND, OR, and NOT.)

Making your statement. Use the words from your Boolean logic map and show how you would use those words together in a search statement.

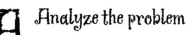

Being ObservANT
Research Planning

Write your research topic here:

A Analyze the problem

- (SIK "Stuff I Know"):

- (SINK "Stuff I Need to Know"):

N Nothing is something: (List all your keywords from your topic, then make a list of any other words you might use if the keywords don't work.) (Think of broader and narrower categories, remember the pyramid.)

T Think of all your possibilities. (Draw a Boolean logic map(s) of the keywords that you will use to do an electronic search on your topic and then show how you would use those words together in a search statement.)

H Hunt for answers. (Make a list of the areas of the library you will need to investigate to research your topic.)

I Isolate/Interpret. Time to take a step back and reflect on your direction. How are you doing? What discoveries have you found? Record some of the ways you have searched.

L Learn direction by reflection. What did you look under that was not helpful? What did you look under that was helpful?

L Link it all together. When you first started your research, were you excited about your topic? Explain. Have you changed your mind? Explain what helped to change your mind.

Handout: Preparing Your Oral Presentation

You have finished gathering all your information and now it is time to link it all together into a three-minute oral presentation. So far you have been gathering information. Now you must take this information and make sense out of it. You have found many theories in your hunt for answers. This mystery has never been solved or it would not still be a real life mystery. It is important that you decide what theory you most agree with, or perhaps after all your research you have found a theory that no one else has yet offered.

There Are Three Elements to a Good Speech:

1. Introduction (or beginning)
2. Body (or middle)
3. Conclusion (or end)

There Are Three Reasons to Give a Speech:

1. To entertain (make the audience laugh)
2. To inform (provide facts about a topic)
3. To persuade (to convince the audience)

Your speech will mostly be to inform. Many speeches have elements of all three, but you must stick to your focus. If you include bits of entertainment your audience will be more eager to connect to your presentation. Entertainment might be a personal story to which the audience could relate. Bringing a part of yourself to the speech helps your audience engage with what you want to say, but it should somehow tie to the information you want to inform them about.

How Do You Begin?

1. Make an outline of all the information you have gathered.
2. Develop note cards from your outline.
3. Do not write everything you want to say on your note cards; use only keywords that will remind you of what you want to say. Number your note cards so that they stay in order.
4. Work on a good introduction that will grab the audience's attention. You may want to write out your entire introduction especially if you are quoting.
5. The body of your speech will contain the information that you want your audience to know about your mystery topic. You will present your main ideas and supporting details here.
6. The conclusion will be where you present the theory that you most agree with. Again, you may want to write out your entire conclusion, especially if you are quoting. Having a good conclusion is important because you want your audience to know that you have reached the end. You do not want to leave your audience hanging; they should know without a doubt that you are finished saying what you set out to tell them.

7. As you start to practice what you are going to say, remember to use good transition words like: therefore, further, in addition, and in conclusion.

8. Do not read your presentation like a report, which is boring to your audience.

9. You should not memorize. That is scary. You might think you have everything memorized but when you get up in front of your audience and see them looking back at you, you may forget what you wanted to say.

10. Think of any visual or audio that you might want to include. If you use these things in your presentation they should add to what you want to say and not be a distraction. If you are using a visual you should refer to it during your speech.

Preparation takes practice.

PRACTICE in the mirror. PRACTICE to your cat.

PRACTICE to your pillow. PRACTICE into a tape recorder.

PRACTICE for your family.

PRACTICE with a friend.

Handout: The Day Has Arrived. Things You Should Remember.

1. **Dress for success**. Look good and you will feel good. If you are presenting as a news reporter, watch the news and see how they dress.
2. **Body language** is important. Stand up straight. Do not swing and sway. Do not play with jewelry or hair.
3. Have **good eye contact**. Look at your audience. If you are using note cards with only keywords listed you will be able to glance down occasionally to remind you of the next thing you want to say. If you write everything out you will be tempted to read and will not be able to have good eye contact.
4. **Vocal quality** is important. You need to speak loudly enough so that your audience can hear you. If you speak too softly your audience will quit trying to listen to you.
5. **Visuals** should add to what you have to say, not cause a distraction. If you are using a visual make sure that it can be seen by the audience and that you refer to it.

You Have Worked Hard to Gather Your Information,
Now You Get the Opportunity to Share What You Have Learned.
Have Fun. Be Creative.

Media Center Crime Solvers

Mystery in the Media Center

Captains _____ and _____

would like to congratulate you on your accomplishments

as a Detective on the case of your real life mystery.

This certifies that_____

has been promoted to Lieutenant Inspector
at
Information Headquarters

Captain_____   Date:_____

Captain_____   Date:_____

GUIDED RESEARCH
in MIDDLE SCHOOL
Mystery in the Media Center

Detective's Casebook

Being ObservANT

A	N	T	H	I	L	L
Analyze	Nothing is something	Think of all your possibilities	Hunt for answers	Isolate/ Interpret	Learn direction by reflection	Link it all together

Qualities of Being a Good Detective

Being ObservANT

> *Searching can be as easy as one-two-three*
> *Being observANT is made to help you see.*
> *That analyzing your topic is the best way to begin*
> *And when you find "nothing," look again*
> *It may be the "something" you never thought of before*
> *That helps you solve your problem, so try once more.*
> *Put your words together in just the right way*
> *Think of your possibilities, everything will be OK.*

Step 1

Analyze your problem.

Ask yourself questions (SIK="Stuff I Know").

What do I already know about my topic before I begin my investigation?

What is my case assignment? What do I need to do to complete my investigation?

Step 2

Nothing is something. Keep a cool head even when it seems you are finding nothing. Think of other ways to search, use new words, or use different sources. Your vocabulary will change as you learn more about your topic. This new knowledge and the new words you learn will guide you to try new searches. You might even change your approach or direction.

Step 3

Think of all your possibilities. Think of what you want to find out about your topic. Do not get bogged down in things that are not working. Thinking about the things you want to find out about your topic will help guide you and keep you focused. Think about how you want to present your information in the end (SINK="Stuff I Need to Know").

Ants build hills.

Hunt for answers. You will be gathering your information from four different areas of the library media center. The areas are: Reference, Nonfiction, Print media, and Electronic resources (Internet and databases).

Isolate/Interpret. What/who is involved in my mystery? What are the theories? What theory do I agree with? While you are gathering clues, you should be thinking about how you are going to present your information and what facts you need to accomplish this task. You may find that your original plan was a good one, but many times you will have to go back and gather different pieces of evidence. You will need to ask yourself if the source you gathered your information from has answered your questions. A detective examines the case from many directions because:

- More information might be needed
- The information already found might lead to new questions
- The clues found have led the detective off track

Learn direction by reflection. Do I need to take a new direction? Are there any questions I still have? This is the time to reflect on where I am now and where I still need to go. This is the time you need to ask yourself if the strategies you have been using are working or do you need to try something else. What have you learned about doing research? Are you focused on the questions you started with?

Link it all together. Once you have gathered your information, you will want to ensure that it is accurate, and you should begin to see that all phases of the investigative process are linked together.
Your case will be filled with questions. Do not get discouraged!

NOTHING IS SOMETHING...
JUST TAKE ONE STEP
AT A TIME!

Be an LMC Detective

You are now a Library Media Center (LMC) Crime Solver. During your investigation you will be reporting to Captains _____ and _____ at Information Headquarters. You will be investigating a real life mystery topic. Your investigation will require you to use five sources from four different areas of the LMC.

Figure 24: Tools of the Trade

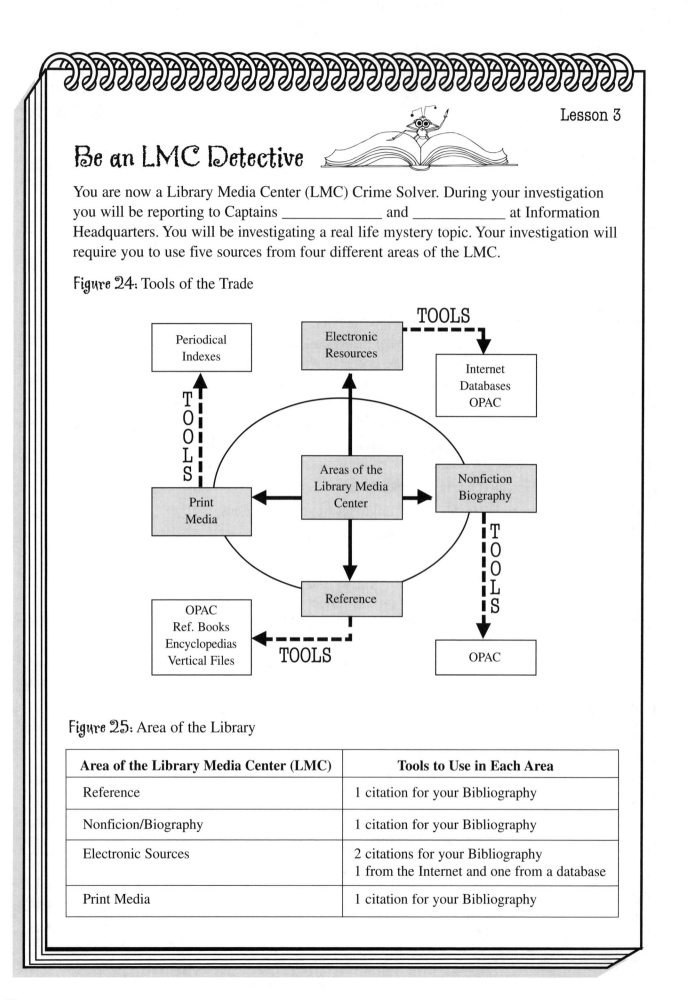

Figure 25: Area of the Library

Area of the Library Media Center (LMC)	Tools to Use in Each Area
Reference	1 citation for your Bibliography
Nonficion/Biography	1 citation for your Bibliography
Electronic Sources	2 citations for your Bibliography 1 from the Internet and one from a database
Print Media	1 citation for your Bibliography

You will use this casebook to record important facts about your mystery. You will collect your information and make a copy or printout of all the materials you collect. You will look at all the theories about your unsolved mystery that will help you come to your own conclusions as an ace on the case. After you have gathered all your clues, you will make an outline of your investigation, prepare a bibliography, and report back to information headquarters to put on a three-minute oral presentation about your topic. You will use cue cards for presenting your topic. Your casebook will help you plan your search as you develop strategies for questioning and gathering clues about your topic. This casebook will provide you with the necessary tools for completing your assignment.

Analyze the problem. Ask yourself questions. In your own words use the rest of this page to summarize what you must do to complete this assignment. Make sure to include information from the chart as you describe all you must do to complete your mystery case.

_____

_____

_____

_____

_____

_____

_____

_____

_____

_____

_____

_____

_____

SIK "Stuff I Know"

Understanding what you already know and what you need to know is the first step in solving your mystery. To be a good detective there will be many important questions you must ask during your mystery solvers case assignment.

Write your topic here and circle the keywords in the topic sentence.

Write a complete sentence on something you already know about your topic:

Circle Your Keywords

Write a complete sentence on something you already know about your topic:

Circle Your Keywords

Write a complete sentence on something you already know about your topic:

Circle Your Keywords

Make a list of the keywords you circled in the sentences above.

Nothing is something. If your keywords above do not work, what words could you use instead? Make a list of the new words you might use. Consider using synonyms. You may use dictionaries, thesauri, biographical dictionaries, or even encyclopedias.

Broad Topic to Narrow Topic: Building the Pyramid

Knowing what categories to look under will help you in your investigation.

Write your complete topic, word for word in the Topic Concept Map below. Map your topic by filling in the bubbles provided—Event, Person, Thing, Place. Think of describing words as appropriate. Everyone will have an event; some will have a person, some a thing, and some will have both. Fill in the bubbles according to the information in your topic.

Fill in the pyramid using your topic. An example of building the pyramid from the top down would be: Mary Celeste at the top of the pyramid, Mystery Ship, Famous Ship, Ships. This example goes from the top down or from the narrow category to the broad category. If you do not know anything about your topic or how to build your pyramid, you may need to look in an encyclopedia or biographical dictionary to get some background information. Understanding broad and narrow categories will help you look for answers. Not everyone will be able to build the pyramid all the way to the bottom, but you will want to try to go as far down as you can.

Figure 7: Topic Concept Map Table

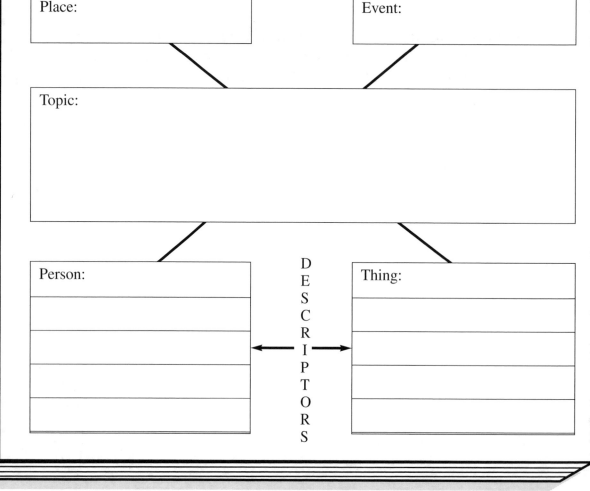

Figure 8: Pyramid

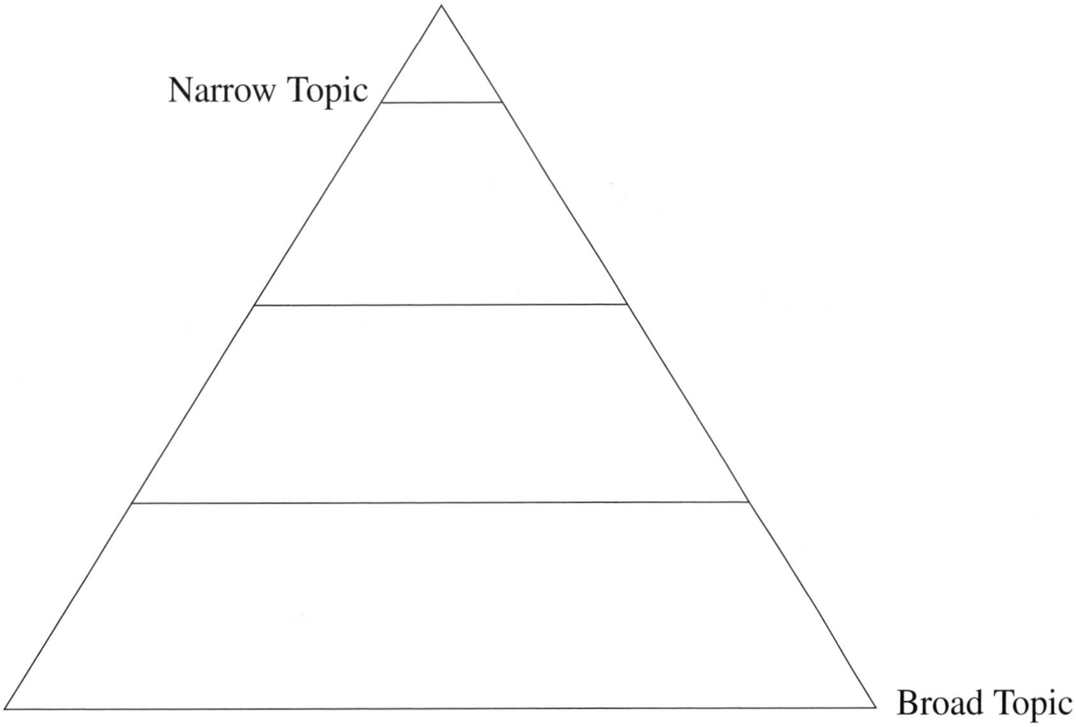

Narrow Topic

Broad Topic

Think of all your possibilities.

Think of what you want to find out about your topic.
Think about how you will want to present your information in the end.

SINK ("Stuff I Need To Know")

It is now time for you to convert the information you already know into useful knowledge. Really think about your topic and all the things you might discover as you begin to do your research. What do you want to find out? Write as many "I Wonder" statements as you can that will help you begin to think about what you want to know.

- I wonder who?
- I wonder what?
- I wonder how?
- I wonder what if?

Use the rest of the page to create "I Wonder" statements that will help guide you as you gather clues.

_____

_____

_____

_____

_____

_____

_____

_____

_____

Figure 26: Hunt for Answers Checklist

Library Media Center Crime Solver:
Hunting for Answers Checklist

✓ here when ALL done	**One citation from Reference** ■ Make a copy of your information_____ ■ Highlight keywords_____ ■ Complete Scene of the Crime Log Sheets_____ ■ Summarize_____ ■ EYE Pages ("I Wonder" and Isolate/Interpret)_____
	One citation from Nonfiction ■ Make a copy of your information_____ ■ Highlight keywords_____ ■ Complete Scene of the Crime Log Sheets_____ ■ Summarize_____ ■ EYE Pages ("I Wonder" and Isolate/Interpret)_____
	One citation from Electronic Resources from the Internet ■ Make a copy of your information_____ ■ Highlight keywords_____ ■ Complete Scene of the Crime Log Sheets_____ ■ Summarize_____ ■ EYE Pages ("I Wonder" and Isolate/Interpret)_____
	One citation from Electronic Resources from a database ■ Make a copy of your information_____ ■ Highlight keywords_____ ■ Complete Scene of the Crime Log Sheets_____ ■ Summarize_____ ■ EYE Pages ("I Wonder" and Isolate/Interpret)_____
	One citation from Print Media ■ Make a copy of your information_____ ■ Highlight keywords_____ ■ Complete Scene of the Crime Log Sheets_____ ■ Summarize _____ ■ EYE Pages ("I Wonder" and Isolate/Interpret)_____

Reference Sources: Scene of the Crime Log Sheet

Hunt for answers

List all keywords you search under to find your topic and record your results in the grid below.

Remember **Nothing Is Something**.

If you look under one topic and find nothing, put on your thinking cap and look again.

Encyclopedia Article		
Keyword List	Found Nothing	Found Something

What keyword, in the index volume, did you use to find your information?

Editor *(First and Last Name)*	
Title of the encyclopedia	
Title of the article in the encyclopedia	
Page numbers of the article	
City of publication	
Publisher's name	
Year of publication *(YYYY)*	
Volume number used	

Reference Book	

Show your OPAC search here:

Call Number:

Author *(Last Name, First Name)*	
Title of book	
City of publication	
Publisher's name	
Year of publication (YYYY)	

Figure 27: Reference Citation Table

Reference Sources

You should have made a *copy* of your reference material. Read and *highlight* the material you have copied. Remember to highlight keywords only and *circle* long passages. *Code* (check mark, star, or asterisk) important dates, names, or other key items you want to remember. In the space below summarize what you have read in your reference source. Use complete sentences.

What is the main idea in the article?

Write about three supporting details that you read in the article.

List three new keywords that you found in this source that will help you find additional information somewhere else.

I = Isolate/Interpret

Look back at your "I Wonder" statements 👁 . Has this source helped you answer any of your questions or statements? Think about what you have read about in this source. What are the theories presented about your mystery? Do you agree with the theories? Why or why not? Journal about your conclusions on this page.

_____

_____

_____

_____

_____

_____

_____

_____

_____

_____

_____

_____

_____

_____

_____

_____

_____

Nonfiction: Scene of the Crime Log Sheet

Hunt for answers

List all keywords you search under to find your topic and record your results in the grid below.

Remember **Nothing Is Something**.

If you look under one topic and find nothing put on your thinking cap and look again.

Nonfiction Book		
Keyword List	Found Nothing	Found Something

Show your OPAC search here:

Call Number:

Author *(Last Name, First Name)*	
Title of book *(will be underlined)*	
City of publication *(followed by colon)*	
Publisher's name *(followed by colon)*	
Year of publication *(YYYY)*	

Nonfiction Book		
Keyword List	Found Nothing	Found Something

Show your OPAC search here:

Call Number:

Author *(Last Name, First Name)*	
Title of book *(will be underlined)*	
City of publication *(followed by colon)*	
Publisher's name *(followed by colon)*	
Year of publication (YYYY)	

Figure 28: Nonfiction Citation Table

Nonfiction Source

You should have made a *copy* of your nonfiction material. Read and *highlight* the material you have copied. Remember to highlight keywords only and *circle* long passages. *Code* (check mark, star, or asterisk) important dates, names, or other key items you want to remember. In the space below summarize what you have read in your nonfiction source. Use complete sentences.

What is the main idea in the article?

Write about three supporting details that you read in the article.

List three new keywords that you found in this source that will help you find additional information somewhere else.

I = Isolate/Interpret

Look back at your "I Wonder" statements 👁. Has this source helped you answer any of your questions or statements? Think about what you have read about in this source. What are the theories presented about your mystery? Do you agree with the theories? Why or why not? Journal about your conclusions on this page.

L (Learn From Your Mistakes—Direction By Reflection)

Use the space provided to journal about your work on your mystery case. What have you learned so far? What words or topics did you look under that were not helpful? What words or topics did you look under that were helpful? Are you becoming a better detective? What new ways have you discovered about how to search for information that are helping you to be more observant?

Figure 29: Making Your Statement

Making Your Statement

INTERNET SEARCH STRATEGY	Number of Results
Try again. This time use good search strategies (AND, OR, + , Quotes) Show search strategy:	
Are there other words you would like to try? Show your search:	
Try again. This time use a database. Database Name:_____ Show search strategy:	
Do you want to try again in the same database or another database using other words? Database Name:_____ Show search strategy:	

Print out one good Internet Article and one good database article. Read your print outs and highlight keywords as you read. Have you found any new words you might try using? YES_____   NO_____

Make a list of your new words.

Electronic Resources (Online Database): Scene of the Crime Log Sheet

Hunt for answers

List all keywords you search under to find your topic and record your results in the grid below.

Remember **Nothing Is Something**.

If you look under one topic and find nothing put on your thinking cap and look again.

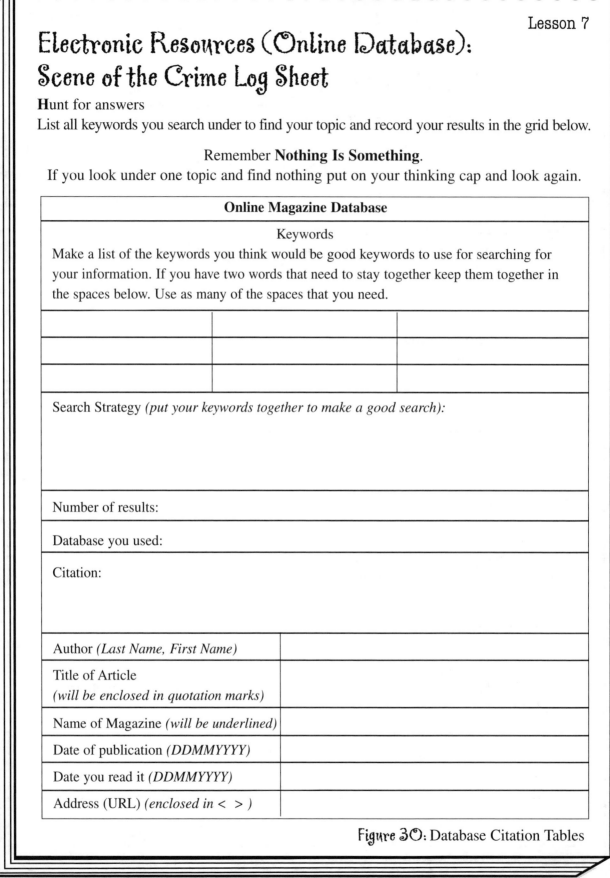

Online Magazine Database		
Keywords Make a list of the keywords you think would be good keywords to use for searching for your information. If you have two words that need to stay together keep them together in the spaces below. Use as many of the spaces that you need.		
Search Strategy *(put your keywords together to make a good search):*		
Number of results:		
Database you used:		
Citation:		
Author *(Last Name, First Name)*		
Title of Article *(will be enclosed in quotation marks)*		
Name of Magazine *(will be underlined)*		
Date of publication *(DDMMYYYY)*		
Date you read it *(DDMMYYYY)*		
Address (URL) *(enclosed in < >)*		

Figure 30: Database Citation Tables

Online Database Source

You should have made a printout (*copy*) of your database material. Read and *highlight* the material you have printed. Remember to highlight keywords only and *circle* long passages. *Code* (check mark, star, or asterisk) important dates, names, or other key items you want to remember. In the space below summarize what you have read in your database source. Use complete sentences.

What is the main idea in the article?

Write about three supporting details that you read in the article.

List three new keywords that you found in this source that will help you find additional information somewhere else.

I = Isolate/Interpret

Look back at your "I Wonder" statements . Has this source helped you answer any of your questions or statements? Think about what you have read about in this source. What are the theories presented about your mystery? Do you agree with the theories? Why or why not? Journal about your conclusions on this page.

Electronic Resources (Internet): Scene of the Crime Log Sheet

Hunt for answers

List all keywords you search under to find your topic and record your results in the grid below.

Remember **Nothing Is Something**.

If you look under one topic and find nothing put on your thinking cap and look again.

Internet
Keywords
Make a list of the keywords you think would be good keywords to use for searching for your information. If you have two words that need to stay together keep them together in the spaces below. Use as many of the spaces that you need.

Search Strategy *(put your keywords together to make a good search):*

Number of results:

Citation

Remember that looking at a Web site is like opening up a file cabinet. Inside the drawer you will find a folder and in that folder will be a document. You might have to look at more than one page to figure out the full citation.

Author *(Last Name, First Name)*	
Title of the Web page *(will be enclosed in quotation marks)*	
Group title *(is there a home page you need to look at?) (will be underlined)*	
Name of Magazine *(will be underlined)*	
Date of publication *(DDMMYYYY)*	
Date you read it *(DDMMYYYY)*	
Address (URL) *(enclosed in < >)*	

Figure 31: Internet Citation Table

Internet Source

You should have made a printout (*copy*) of your Internet source material. Read and *highlight* the material you have printed. Remember to highlight keywords only and *circle* long passages. *Code* (check mark, star, or asterisk) important dates, names, or other key items you want to remember. In the space below summarize what you have read from your Internet source. Use complete sentences.

What is the main idea in the article?

Write about three supporting details that you read in the article.

List three new keywords that you found in this source that will help you find additional information somewhere else.

I = Isolate/Interpret

Look back at your "I Wonder" statements  . Has this source helped you answer any of your questions or statements? Think about what you have read about in this source. What are the theories presented about your mystery? Do you agree with the theories? Why or why not? Journal about your conclusions on this page.

_____

_____

_____

_____

_____

_____

_____

_____

_____

_____

_____

_____

_____

_____

_____

_____

_____

_____

Figure 32: Web Evaluation

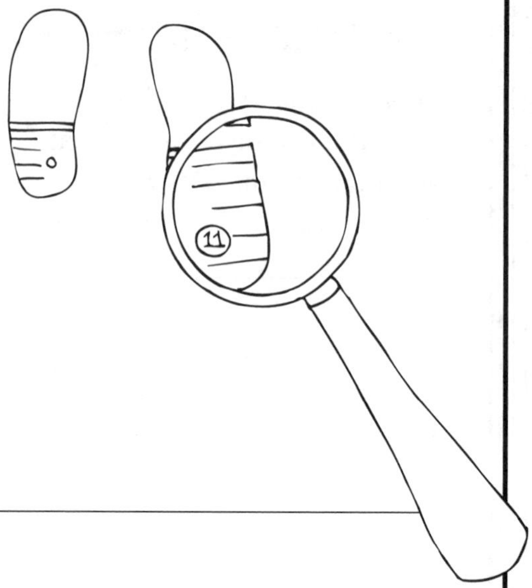

Being A Cyber Snoop

Web Evaluation

Name of the page _____

URL: _____

http:// _____

Domain Name _____

When was the page created? _____

When was the page updated? _____

Who is responsible for creating/maintaining the page? _____

Was the author's e-mail address included on the page? ☐ YES ☐ NO

If you can link back to the main page, what is the main page's URL?

http:// _____

I can read and understand most or all of the words at this Web site ☐ YES ☐ NO

Is the information I found at this site current and up-to-date? ☐ YES ☐ NO

★ Web Evaluation sheet should be used with Lesson 10

Print Media (Newspapers, Magazines, etc.): Scene of the Crime Log Sheet

Hunt for answers

List all keywords you search under to find your topic and record your results in the grid below.

Remember **Nothing Is Something**.

If you look under one topic and find nothing put on your thinking cap and look again.

Periodicals		
Keywords Make a list of the keywords you think would be good keywords to use for searching for your information. Use as many of the spaces as you need.		
What Periodical Index did you use?		
Citation		
Author *(Last Name, First Name)*		
Title of Article *(will be in quotation marks)*		
Name of Magazine *(will be underlined)*		
Date of publication *(DDMMYYYY)*		
Page numbers		
Did you find your periodical and article on the shelf?	Yes	No
If you answered no to the question above you will need to try and find your article in an online magazine database.		

Figure 33: Periodical Citation Table

Print Media Source

You should have made a *copy* of your material you have gathered from a periodical, magazine, or newspaper. Read and *highlight* the material you have copied. Remember to highlight keywords only and *circle* long passages. *Code* (check mark, star, or asterisk) important dates, names, or other key items you want to remember. In the space below summarize what you have read in your print media source. Use complete sentences.

What is the main idea in the article?

Write about three supporting details that you read in the article.

List three new keywords that you found in this source that will help you find additional information somewhere else.

I = Isolate/Interpret

Look back at your "I Wonder" statements  . Has this source helped you answer any of your questions or statements? Think about what you have read about in this source. What are the theories presented about your mystery? Do you agree with the theories? Why or why not? Journal about your conclusions on this page.

Learn Direction by Reflection

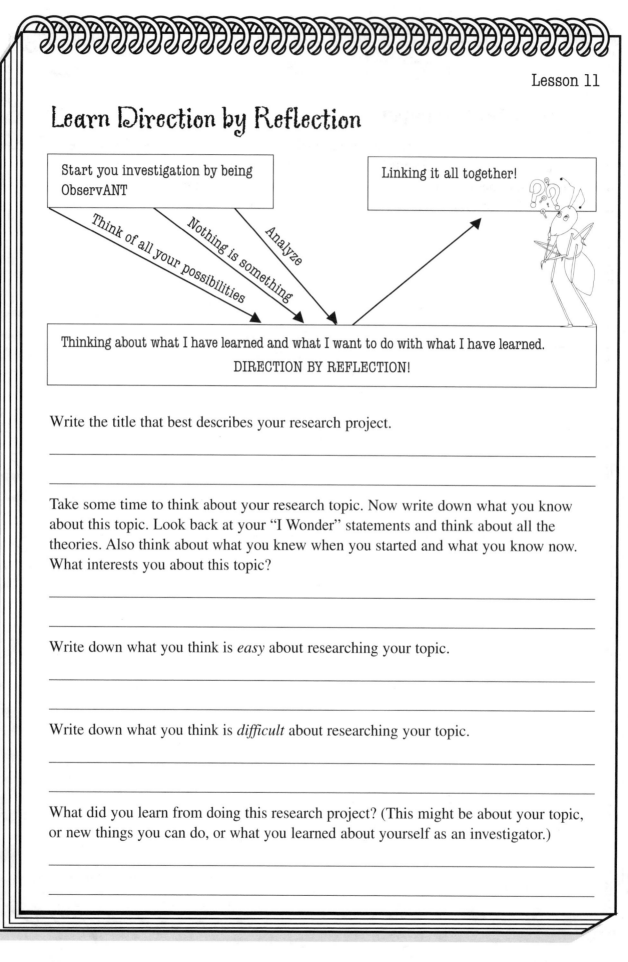

Start you investigation by being ObservANT

Linking it all together!

Think of all your possibilities

Nothing is something

Analyze

Thinking about what I have learned and what I want to do with what I have learned.
DIRECTION BY REFLECTION!

Write the title that best describes your research project.

_____

_____

Take some time to think about your research topic. Now write down what you know about this topic. Look back at your "I Wonder" statements and think about all the theories. Also think about what you knew when you started and what you know now. What interests you about this topic?

_____

_____

Write down what you think is *easy* about researching your topic.

_____

_____

Write down what you think is *difficult* about researching your topic.

_____

_____

What did you learn from doing this research project? (This might be about your topic, or new things you can do, or what you learned about yourself as an investigator.)

_____

_____

Linking It All Together

Questioning is the key to solving your case.
In complete sentences answer the following questions about your case:

Who?

_____

_____

_____

What?

_____

_____

_____

Where?

_____

_____

_____

When?

_____

_____

_____

Why?

_____

_____

_____

How?

_____

_____

_____

What I Learned

(Where there is a will there is a way)
What have you learned by snooping through the material on your mysterious topic?
Using complete sentences, record three facts that you have learned that you did not
know before about your topic:

_____

_____

_____

_____

_____

Using complete sentences, record three questions that you might still have about your topic:

_____

_____

_____

_____

_____

Where else might you look for information?

_____

_____

Now you are ready to present your case.

A	N	T	H	I	L	L
Analyze	Nothing is something	Think of all your possibilities	Hunt for answers	Isolate/ Interpret	Learn direction by reflection	Link it all together

Recommended Reading

Citing Your Work and Giving Credit (Plagiarism and Copyright)

Abilock, Debbie. *Noodletools*. 2006. Noodletools, Inc. 12 Apr. 2006 <http://www.noodletools.com>.

Online interactive tools designed to help students and professionals with their online research. Tools are both free and subscription-based and provide help in selecting a search engine and finding relevant sources to help with citing those sources in MLA or APA style. Includes help for both teachers and students.

Simpson, Carol. *Copyright for Schools: A Practical Guide*. 4th ed. Worthington, OH: Linworth Publishing, Inc., 2005.

Discusses copyright law in relation to schools. Covers issues relating to specific kinds of medium. Each section of the book presents activities that occur in school settings.

Warlick, David. *Landmark's Son of Citation Machine*. Apr. 2006. The Landmark Project. 28 June 2006 <http://citationmachine.net>.

Interactive tool developed to help teachers model proper use of information property.

Critical and Creative Thinking Skills

The 21st Century Learning Initiative. *Adolescence: A Critical Evolutionary Adaptation*. Bath, U.K.: The 21st Century Learning Initiative, Draft Jan. 13, 2005. 28 June 2006 <http://www.21learn.org/arch/articles/adoles_crit_evo_adapt.doc>.

Examines where current theories of education come from and the confusion between schooling and learning. This paper looks at the ever-increasing concern that formal education is failing to prepare young people for adult life and responsibilities. This paper argues that by having a better understanding of the biological processes involved in human learning as it connects to cultural practices, perhaps formal educational practices can be transformed.

Black, Susan. "Teaching Students to Think Critically." *Education Digest* (Feb. 2005): 42-48.

Offers advice on developing and teaching critical thinking in students with suggestions for incorporating several skills into daily instruction. Offers several opinions about really implementing critical thinking into the classroom and is a condensed article from *American School Board Journal*, 191 December (2004), 52-54.

Brandt, Ron. "On Using Knowledge: A Conversation with Bob Sylwester" *Educational Leadership,* (Mar. 1997): 16-19. Master File Premier. EBSCO. Avenel Middle School Media Center, NJ. 4 May 2004 <http://search.epnet.com/>.

This paper is an interview with author Bob Sylwester discussing his perspectives on using knowledge and about the human brain. Also included is a discussion on the application of brain research in schools using brain-compatible teaching and practical applications of neuroscience.

Cohen, Daniel. *Creativity, What Is It?* New York: M. Evans and Company, Inc., 1977.

This book in based on the premise that creativity can be understood as a function of the brain but that high intelligence and being highly creative are not necessarily the same. There is some degree of creativity in all of us and that creativity cannot flourish in a vacuum, so we must develop or allow social conditions that will encourage creativity.

de Bono, Edward. *de Bono's Thinking Course*. New York: Facts on File, 1994.

Guide to thinking. Learning to look at problems and considering a variety of alternatives to find the solution. This book is really designed so that you could use the strategies to actually put together a thinking club. Thinking is looked at in connection to emotions and values, on ways of doing things, on targets, on developing deliberate thinking, and on thinking about thinking.

de Bono, Edward. *Lateral Thinking: Creativity Step By Step*. New York: Harper & Row, 1970.

A practical guide to creative thinking. de Bono looks at two ways of thinking, lateral and vertical. Vertical thinking is described as logical, moving from one step to another to one correct solution. Lateral thinking, on the other hand, is shown as an insight that can be learned, just like any other skill, solving problems from within by rearrangement of information. Lateral thinking is not about how to collect information but how to use information to restructure knowledge. Lateral thinking is the generation of new ideas. This book provides an explanation of lateral thinking and gives examples and opportunities for practicing this skill.

Thompson, Charles. *What a Great Idea!: Key Steps Creative People Take*. New York: HarperPerrenial, 1992.

Chic Thompson is the president of the Creative Management Group and is an adjunct faculty member at several universities and institutes and a presenter all over the world for corporations, etc. This book is a workbook designed to challenge the assumptions you may hold that might stifle your creativity.

van Gelder, Tim. "Teaching Critical Thinking: Some Lessons from Cognitive Science." *College Teaching* (Winter 2005): 41-46.

Six key lessons from cognitive science for teachers of critical thinking are looked at and the article provides some guidelines for teaching in light of these lessons.

Information Literacy Standards

AASL/AECT. *Information Literacy Standards for Student Learning*. Chicago: American Library Association and the Association for Educational Communication and Technology, 1998.

Presents the new information literacy standards separate from *Information Power: Building Partnerships for Learning*. Easy reference guide.

AASL/AECT. *Information Power: Building Partnerships for Learning*. Chicago: American Library Association and the Association for Educational Communication and Technology, 1998.

Presents lesson plans designed to help secondary school librarians guide their students through the research process. Each lesson includes instructions, reproducibles, and a bibliography. The practical ideas can easily be adapted for a specific grade, curriculum, or reference collection. Includes information literacy standards for student learning.

Inquiry Based Learning and Brain Research

CISSL (Center of International Scholarship in School Libraries). Directors, Ross Todd and Carol C. Kuhlthau. 1 May 2006. 4 July 2006 <http://cissl.scils.rutgers.edu/>. (Participant in New Jersey Study, 2004).

CISSL is the Center of International Scholarship in School Libraries and is dedicated to research, scholarship, education, and consultancy for school library professionals. CISSL is focused on conducting research and developing strategies for school libraries to replicate and implement. They are focused on the impact of inquiry-based learning. This Web site shows their mission, how to link to other research, and how to become involved in the Center and the research studies in which they are involved

Donham, Jean, et al. *Inquiry-Based Learning: Lessons from Library Power*. Professional Growth Series. Worthington, OH: Linworth Publishing, Inc., 2001.

Inquiry implies involvement that leads to understanding—real life questioning that leads to understanding. The authors use case studies to provide strategies and examples of how to use the Library Power initiative to regenerate teaching and learning.

Dyck, Brenda. "Hovering: Teaching the Adolescent Brain!" Online posting. *The MiddleWeb Listserv*. 4 July 2006 <http://www.middleweb.com/MWLISTCONT/MSLhovering.html>.

This article on MiddleWeb listserv discusses brain research and the idea of "hovering" as presented by Dr. Sylwester. Hovering is the idea that middle school students need someone walking beside them during their learning processes even at a time when they want to differentiate themselves from adults. Hovering is compared to the idea of apprenticeships where the apprentice learns from the mentor.

Kuhlthau, Carol C. *Seeking Meaning: A Process Approach to Library and Information Services*. 2nd ed. Westport, CT: Libraries Unlimited, 2004.

This book is the updated edition of Dr. Kuhlthau's work from about 10 years ago, and it is wonderful to see her work and practice since then. This edition incorporates not only the work the author has done since 1993, but also related work by other researchers. She describes actions or intervention zones undertaken at different stages in the search process and the associated feelings. Focusing on human information behavior she provides effective intervention strategies that can be used to help students move through the research process.

Lau Whelan, Debra. "13,000 Kids Can't Be Wrong." *School Library Journal* (Feb. 2004): 46-51.

This article examines the Ohio Study: Student Learning Through Ohio Schools, implemented by the Center for International Scholarship in School Libraries and conducted by Dr. Ross Todd and Dr. Carol C. Kuhlthau. This study shows how school libraries really help students learn. The study's findings are included along with student voices and a profile of a successful school library.

Sylwester, Robert. *A Biological Brain in a Cultural Classroom: Enhancing Cognitive and Social Development Through Collaborative Classroom Management*. New York: Crown Press, 2003.

Explains how the latest biological research findings can be applied to student-teacher dynamics in the classroom. Discusses new information about how the brain works and how this knowledge can help teachers better prepare their students for learning.

The Middle School Student and Tools to Use

Information Powered Schools. Ed. Susan Hughes-Hassell and Ann Wheelock. Chicago: Public Education Network and American Association of School Libraries/ALA, 2001.

This is a "how to" manual for administrators, teachers, and school library media specialists. It includes numerous forms, ideas, and helpful advice for building a collaborative environment where the school library media center is at the heart of the school.

Kasowitz, Abby B. *Using the Big6™ to Teach and Learn with the Internet.* Worthington, OH: Linworth Publishing, Inc., 2000.

Designed as an instructional guide for teaching and learning using the Internet, this book has many examples and guidelines that will guide in the development of your own lessons while using the Internet.

Logan, Debra Kay. *Information Skills Toolkit: Collaborative Integrated Instruction for the Middle Grades.* Worthington, OH: Linworth Publishing, Inc., 2000.

This book is a working toolkit filled with lesson ideas and worksheets to teach and adapt integrated subject area and information skills lessons designed for the middle grades curriculum.

Middle School Journal. National Middle School Association.

This journal publishes findings of research related to middle grades and focuses on key issues for teaching the various disciplines.

Stanley, Deborah B. *Practical Steps to the Research Process for Middle School.* Englewood, CO: Libraries Unlimited, 2003.

This is a step-by-step, practical guide for teaching the research process.

Valenza, Joyce Kasman. *Power Tools: 100+ Essential Forms and Presentations for Your School Library Information Program.* Chicago: American Library Association, 1998.

This book is filled with wonderful reproducibles and an accompanying CD-ROM that includes PowerPoint presentations and the ability to download templates, etc. from the CD. A must have in school libraries.

Public Speaking

Otfinoski, Steven. *Speaking Up, Speaking Out: A Kid's Guide to Making Speeches, Oral Reports, and Conversation.* Brookfield, CT: Millbrook Press, 1996.

Breaks down the art of public speaking into steps. Helps students learn to take good notes as they gather information for their presentation. He discusses types of speeches and the organization of a good speech. Good for students and teachers alike.

Search Models

Eisenberg, Michael B., and Robert E. Berkowitz. *Information Problem-Solving: The Big Six Skills Approach to Library & Information Skills Instruction.* Norwood, NJ: Ablex Publishing Corporation, 1990.

The Big6™ is an information literacy model focused on a general problem-solving approach to library and information skills instruction. This book covers how to apply this scaffolding process to research and learning.

Kuhlthau, Carol C. *Teaching the Library Research Process: A Step-By-Step Program for Secondary School Students*. Nyak, NY: Center for Applied Research in Education, 1985.

Through case studies, Dr. Kuhlthau tracks student progress using observation of search strategies and interviews and by examining student search journals. Attitudinal and emotional aspects of the inquiry process are stressed. Dr. Kuhlthau developed a search process model that is made up of the stages students go through during the information search process. A classic in the information seeking process literature.

Yucht, Alice. *Flip It!* Worthington, OH: Linworth Publishing, Inc., 1997.

Presents a framework for teaching research skills and strategies to help students solve problems using the acronym FLIP to define the steps involved. The author adds "It" to the acronym to represent intelligent thinking, something to remind students to always examine and think as they move through any research process.

Technology and Learning

November, Alan. "Teaching Kids to Be Web Literate." *Technology & Learning* (Mar. 2001): 42-44.

Discusses how young minds can be manipulated if they are not schooled in learning to evaluate what they are accessing. He tells a true story of Zach and his search for information about the Holocaust that ended in wrong information. He emphasizes that students need to be taught how to make meaning out of what they find on the Internet not just the skills for accessing information.

Prensky, Marc. *Marc Prensky.com*. 2002. 4 July 2006 <http://www.marcprensky.com/default.asp>.

Makes the case that the students we are teaching today have changed radically; they are not the students we might have been taught to teach. The students we are teaching today have grown up in a digital environment, they do not know life without it, and are adept at multitasking. He calls these students "Digital Natives" and those of us teaching these students "Digital Immigrants." He brings a challenge to educators of this new generation of learners to teach in a different way. His big focus is using digital games as a method of teaching.

Shaffer, David Williamson, et al. "Video Games and the Future of Learning" *Phi Delta Kappan* (Oct. 2005): 105-111.

Authors discuss the power of video games to construct meaning. They look at learning environments and game properties and how the use of games can transform education. They argue that our students will learn from video games. Who will create those games?

Warlick, David. *Redefining Literacy for the 21st Century*. Worthington, OH: Linworth Publishing, Inc., 2004.

The nature of information is changing. What does that mean to the way we process information, learn to read, and express ideas?

Web Site Evaluation

Arnone, Marilyn P. *Website Motivational Analysis Checklist: WebMac Middle*. 1 Mar. 2006. Marilyn P. Arnone. 11 Apr. 2006 <http://www.marilynarnone.com/WebMACMiddle2.0.pdf>.

Barker, Joe. *Evaluating Web Pages: Techniques to Apply & Questions to Ask*. 22 Mar. 2005. The Library-University of California, Berkeley. 4 July 2006 <http://www.lib.berkeley.edu/TeachingLib/Guides/Internet/Evaluate.html>.

Joseph, Linda C. "WWW CyberGuides for Web Evaluation." *Adventures of Cyberbee*. 18 Apr. 2006. 4 July 2006 <http://www.cyberbee.com/guides.html>.

Schrock, Kathleen. *Kathy Schrock's Guide for Educators*. 2006. Discovery Education. 4 July 2006. <http://school.discovery.com/schrockguide/eval.html>.